# BASIC READING INVENTORY

## Second Edition

PRE-PRIMER—GRADE EIGHT

# JERRY L. JOHNS
## NORTHERN ILLINOIS UNIVERSITY

**KENDALL/HUNT PUBLISHING COMPANY**
Dubuque, Iowa, USA • Toronto, Ontario, Canada

Reading Assessment Series

*Consulting Editor*—Lyndon W. Searfoss
*Basic Reading Inventory*—Jerry L. Johns
*Decoding Inventory*—Lyndon W. Searfoss and H. Donald Jacobs
*Content Reading Inventory*—Lana McWilliams and Thomas A. Rakes
*Diagnostic Reading Inventory*—H. Donald Jacobs and Lyndon W. Searfoss

Material on pages 55–71, 85–101, 115–131, as well as Appendix C, may be reproduced without obtaining written permission from the publisher.

C   402315   02

# Contents

# Tables

# Preface to the Second Edition

The Basic Reading Inventory is intended for classroom teachers, for students in preservice education, for teachers taking introductory and advanced reading courses, for reading specialists, for learning disability teachers, for school psychologists, and for school systems desiring to offer inservice work in reading diagnosis. The manual explains how to administer, score, and interpret the Basic Reading Inventory. Also included are graded word lists and graded passages that can be used with students to place them in appropriate reading materials and to determine their strengths and weaknesses in word attack and comprehension. Because this inventory includes numerous examples, strategy lessons, and summary aids, it should enable professionals of diverse training to enhance reading instruction in classrooms, resource rooms, diagnostic centers, and clinics.

The time and energy spent in preparing the second edition of the Basic Reading Inventory has been devoted to refining those components that warranted revision, clarification, expansion, and updating. Users of the first edition will find that the current volume does not depart from the philosophy and procedures originally suggested. The guiding question for any revision was: Will the change improve the inventory? Most of the revisions were suggested by users of the inventory.

The manual is essentially the same and remains a distinguishing feature of the inventory. Several sections have been clarified and/or enlarged. The most notable change is in the suggestions for using the Basic Reading Inventory to enhance instruction. Several strategies are included for analyzing strengths and weaknesses in word attack and comprehension. Greater attention is also given to a systematic way to use miscue analysis.

Several passages in the Basic Reading Inventory have been refined or replaced. Comprehension is now assessed with five different types of comprehension questions, ranging from the literal level to inference and evaluation questions. Analysis of the student's comprehension performance is possible on several levels. Scoring guides have also been added for each passage to make the task of determining reading levels easier. The concept of gray areas between reading levels has been introduced as an aid to help teachers make judgments when necessary. The summary sheet of the performance booklet has been revised to contain more information about the student's reading.

Finally, the annotated sources for further learning have been updated and the summary sheets have been refined and expanded. Teachers and clinicians should welcome these improvements in the appendices.

Although this is the second edition, the Basic Reading Inventory has existed, in one form or another, for over a decade. It has been used with thousands of students in a wide variety of educational settings. As an informal test, the Basic Reading Inventory makes no statistical claims to validity and reliability. The years have provided evidence of its usefulness to a diverse group of professionals who are interested in informally assessing reading performance.

To all those colleagues, students, teachers, and reading specialists who have offered their help, criticism, and encouragement, thank you. Your efforts have helped to improve the second edition of the Basic Reading Inventory.

JLJ

# INTRODUCTION TO THE BASIC READING INVENTORY

# The Teacher's Role in the Improvement of Reading

How can we improve reading instruction? One answer to this question focuses on a search for programs and materials that make better provisions for the varying needs of students. There is ample evidence that an abundance of materials will not insure that all students will become effective readers. The continued search for materials to promote growth in reading may be a misdirected effort; moreover, some authorities claim that such a search conflicts with one of the most outstanding endeavors in reading research. In reporting conclusions from 27 first-grade reading studies, Bond and Dykstra (1967, p. 123) note that:

1. No one approach [to teaching reading] is so distinctly better in all situations and respects than the others that it should be considered the one best method and the one to be used exclusively.
2. The tremendous range among classrooms within any method [of teaching reading] points out the importance of elements in the learning situation over and above the methods employed. To improve reading instruction, it is necessary to train better teachers of reading rather than to expect a panacea in the form of materials.

These conclusions raise a significant concern with regard to the importance of methods and materials used in teaching reading. Since there was greater variation between teachers (within the methods) than there was between the methods, the importance of the teacher's role in the learning process is highlighted. The recurring emphasis on the importance of the teacher is of special interest with regard to the Basic Reading Inventory.

Since the teacher is of crucial importance in most learning environments, it is necessary to place increased emphasis on those instructional strategies generally believed to be essential for effective reading instruction. Perhaps the first step necessary in establishing a successful reading program is the development of some method for diagnosing the specific reading needs of each student (Rutherford, 1971). In short, the teacher needs to: (1) identify those students who are experiencing difficulty in reading; and (2) uncover and study their specific types of reading difficulties so that effective instruction can be given.

The classroom teacher is often in the best position to determine whether or not a student is having difficulty with reading. She* can observe the student daily in a variety of situations. She can note the kinds of miscues he makes, which tasks he can do easily, and what areas cause him difficulty. She can also evaluate the student's ability to apply his reading strategies in various learning tasks occurring in the classroom. Many methods and techniques can be used by teachers to assess a student's strengths and weaknesses in reading. The Basic Reading Inventory is one procedure the classroom teacher can use to evaluate a student's reading performance, place him in appropriate instructional materials, and develop reading strategy lessons.

---

*For the sake of simplicity and consistency, the pronoun *she* will refer to the teacher and *he* will refer to the student. This avoids ambiguity when both teacher and student are referred to in the same sentence.

# Overview of the Basic Reading Inventory

The Basic Reading Inventory, an individually administered informal reading test, is composed of a series of graded word lists and graded passages. Comprehension questions follow each passage. This manual explains the purposes of the Basic Reading Inventory, gives directions for administering and scoring the inventory, and provides concrete assistance for interpreting the findings of the inventory so that the results can be used to improve reading instruction.

Three forms of the Basic Reading Inventory are included so that a variety of purposes can be achieved. One of the three forms of the Basic Reading Inventory may be used to assess a student's oral reading. As the student reads, the teacher notes reading miscues such as mispronunciations of words, omitted words, reversals, repetitions, and substitutions. Another form of the inventory can be used for silent reading. It is important that all students, especially those above the primary grades, engage in silent reading in order to help determine their three reading levels. The remaining form of the inventory can be used either to estimate the student's listening level or as a post-test to evaluate instruction. Teachers are encouraged to use the three forms of the Basic Reading Inventory in a flexible manner so that the student's reading can be evaluated thoroughly.

All passages in the Basic Reading Inventory were evaluated by one or more readability formulas. Such formulas provide one estimate of the difficulty level of reading material. The pre-primer and primer selections were evaluated with the Fry (1968) readability formula. The selections written for grades one through three were evaluated with the Spache (1974) readability formula and the Fry readability formula. The remaining selections were evaluated with the Dale-Chall (1948) readability formula and the Fry readability formula. The readability ratings for the passages in the Basic Reading Inventory are presented in Table 1.

**Table 1**
Readability Ratings for the Three Forms of the Basic Reading Inventory

| Form of Basic Reading Inventory | Readability Formula | Graded Paragraphs | | | | | | | | | |
|---|---|---|---|---|---|---|---|---|---|---|---|
| | | PP | P | 1 | 2 | 3 | 4 | 5 | 6 | 7 | 8 |
| A | Fry | PP | P | 1 | 2 | 3 | 4 | 5 | 6 | 7 | 7 |
| | Spache | | | 1.4 | 2.2 | 2.5 | | | | | |
| | Dale-Chall | | | | | | 4 | 5–6 | 5–6 | 7–8 | 7–8 |
| B | Fry | PP | P | 1 | 2 | 3 | 4 | 5 | 6 | 7 | 8 |
| | Spache | | | 1.4 | 2.1 | 2.9 | | | | | |
| | Dale-Chall | | | | | | 4 | 5–6 | 5–6 | 7–8 | 7–8 |
| C | Fry | PP | P | 1 | 2 | 3 | 4 | 5 | 6 | 7 | 8 |
| | Spache | | | 1.2 | 2.0 | 2.4 | | | | | |
| | Dale-Chall | | | | | | 4 | 5–6 | 5–6 | 7–8 | 7–8 |

Four numerals are used to code the grade level of the word lists and passages in the Basic Reading Inventory. By determining which two numerals are identical, the teacher can determine the grade level of the word list or passage. For example, A 1417 indicates that the word list or passage in Form A is at the first grade level of difficulty; B 8224 indicates that the word list or passage in Form B is at the second grade level of difficulty. A similar procedure is followed for the remaining word lists and passages.

Unlike some published reading inventories, the Basic Reading Inventory does not contain any illustrations to accompany the graded passages. Pictures can make reading material attractive. They can also capture the interest of a student. Pictures, however, sometimes provide clues to help the student understand the passage. Since the Basic Reading Inventory is designed primarily to assess how a student uses *language* cues to reconstruct meaning from print, no illustrations are included. Teachers can be assured that the student is using language cues as he processes the graded passages.

Performance booklets* (one for each student) are used to record a student's performance on the graded word lists and the graded passages. Permission is granted to users of the Basic Reading Inventory to reproduce all, or any part, of the three performance booklets that follow each form of the Basic Reading Inventory.

The three appendices contain sources for further learning, reading strategy lessons, and aids to summarize the test results. The aids contained in Appendix C may be reproduced by users of this inventory.

The validity of a student's performance on the Basic Reading Inventory is directly related to how completely and accurately the teacher is able to record the student's reading miscues and answers to the comprehension questions. As a method of self-checking, the teacher may wish to record the student's reading on a tape recorder.

## Purposes of the Basic Reading Inventory

On the basis of the student's performance on the word lists and graded passages, the teacher can determine the student's:

1. independent reading level—the level at which the student reads fluently with excellent comprehension.
2. instructional reading level—the level at which the student can make maximum progress in reading with teacher guidance.
3. frustration level—the level at which the student is unable to pronounce many of the words and/or is unable to comprehend the material satisfactorily.
4. strengths and weaknesses in word attack—the teacher can evaluate the student's ability to use phonic analysis, context cues, syntax, and structural analysis to pronounce words.
5. strengths and weaknesses in comprehension—the teacher can evaluate the student's ability to answer various types of comprehension questions.

In addition, the teacher may wish to determine the student's:

6. listening level—the highest level of material that the student can comprehend when the material is read to him.

*Spirit duplicating masters are also available for the performance booklets. Contact the publisher.

# Background Information on Reading Levels and the Listening Level

A major function of the Basic Reading Inventory is to identify a student's three reading levels: independent, instructional, frustration. Numerous questions have been raised about standards for evaluating a student's performance on reading inventories (Johns, 1976). While there is some research (Powell, 1971) to indicate that the original criteria suggested by Betts (1954) are too high for determining the instructional level in the primary grades, studies by Pikulski (1974) and Hays (1975) report contradictory findings. In more recent years, Ekwall (1974, 1976) has presented evidence that supports retaining the traditional Betts criteria. Users of the Basic Reading Inventory, however, may wish to be more lenient in using the 95 percent word recognition score in context as the cut-off for the instructional level with primary-grade students. Since the Basic Reading Inventory uses the notion of **significant** miscues for determining word recognition percentages, the Betts criteria are used with some adaptations. Teachers should remember that the numerical criteria for reading levels are not absolute standards; they are guidelines that help teachers evaluate a student's reading. Each of the three reading levels presented below will be considered from two viewpoints: the teacher's and the student's. The listening level will also be discussed.

## What Is the Independent Reading Level?

*Teacher's viewpoint.* The independent reading level is that level at which the student can read fluently without teacher assistance. In other words, the student can read the materials on his own with excellent comprehension. This is the level of supplementary and recreational reading. The material should not cause the student any difficulty. If the student reads orally, his reading should be expressive with accurate attention to punctuation. At this level, the student's reading should be free from finger pointing, vocalizing, lip movement, poor phrasing, and other indications of general tension or problems with the reading material.

In order to be considered at the student's independent level, materials should be read with 99 percent accuracy in terms of word recognition. Even in a situation of oral reading at sight, the student should generally not make more than one significant miscue in each hundred running words. With respect to comprehension, the score should be no lower than 90 percent when a variety of comprehension questions are asked. In short, the student should be able to fully understand the material.

It is important that the above criteria for determining a student's independent reading level be applied with careful teacher judgment. Some of the criteria, especially the 99 percent accuracy for word recognition, may have to be modified somewhat in evaluating a student's performance. The younger reader, for example, may frequently substitute "a" for "the" and vice versa while reading. An older student may omit or substitute a number of words that do not seriously interfere with his fluency and/or understanding of the passage. Miscues of this nature should be regarded as acceptable. If the teacher has correctly determined the student's independent reading level, she can be assured that the student will experience little difficulty with materials which are written at or below that particular level.

*Student's viewpoint.* Since most students have never heard of the various reading levels, they would not use the percentages and related behavioral characteristics described above. A student might, however, describe his independent reading level in these terms: "I can read this book by myself, and I understand what I read. I like reading books like this; they're easy."

## What Is the Instructional Reading Level?

*Teacher's viewpoint.* The instructional reading level is that level at which the student can, theoretically, make maximum growth in reading. It is the level where the student is challenged but not frustrated. Many teachers are interested in finding the student's instructional level so that they can provide classroom reading materials at that level. At the instructional level, the student should be free from externally observable symptoms of difficulty, such as finger pointing, produced by the reading materials. Although the student might experience some difficulties when reading classroom materials at sight, most of these difficulties should be overcome after the student has had an opportunity to read the same material silently. In other words, oral rereading should be definitely improved over oral reading at sight. If the student is to make maximum progress from instruction, he should encounter no more difficulty in reading materials than can be adequately dealt with through good teaching.

In order to be considered at the student's instructional level, materials should be read with 95 percent accuracy in terms of word recognition. Although some difficulties will probably arise in word recognition, the student should be able to use contextual and syntactic clues, phonics, and/or other strategies to unlock most unknown words. In terms of comprehension, the student should achieve a score of at least 75 percent.

It is at the instructional level that the student will have the best opportunity to build new reading strategies. This is the level at which formal reading instruction is likely to be most successful. If students are to be placed in certain books for reading instruction, the teacher should be sure that such books are at their instructional levels.

*Student's viewpoint.* If a student were asked to describe his instructional level, he might say the following: "I can understand what I am taught from this reading book. Some of the words are hard, but after the teacher gives me some help, the story is easy to read. The workbook pages are helping me."

## What Is the Frustration Level?

*Teacher's viewpoint.* The frustration level is that level at which the student should not be given materials to read. A very serious problem in many elementary school classrooms today is that a large number of students are asked to read books at their frustration levels. The student, at his frustration level, is unable to deal with the reading material. There are numerous behavioral characteristics which may be observed if the student is attempting to read materials which are too difficult for him. The student may, in some cases, actually refuse to continue reading the book. He may also exhibit lack of expression in oral reading, lip movement during silent reading, difficulty in pronouncing words, word-by-word reading, and/or finger pointing.

The criteria for the frustration level, in addition to the behavioral characteristics noted above, are word recognition scores of 90 percent or less and comprehension scores of 50 percent or less. For example, a student who could not correctly pronounce 90 or more words in a 100-word selection and who could not answer at least half of the questions asked by the teacher is reading material that is too difficult.

*Student's viewpoint*. Since reading materials at this level are too difficult for the student, it is very likely that he might describe the frustration level in these terms: "Why do you give me books like this to read? They're too hard. I hate to read when books are this hard. I hardly know any of the words. Why don't you give me an easier book?" Other students will say nothing when books are too difficult for them to read, but the perceptive teacher will note when books are at a student's frustration level. The teacher can then provide other materials that are at the student's independent or instructional levels.

## What Is the Listening Level?

The listening level is the **highest** level at which the student can understand material that is read **to** him. Determining this level can help the teacher ascertain whether a student is a disabled reader. When a substantial difference exists between the student's instructional level and listening level (generally a year or more), it usually indicates that the student is a disabled reader who should be able to make significant growth in his reading achievement. The larger the difference, the more reason for the teacher to believe that the student can profit from special instruction in reading.

The criteria for the listening level are a minimum comprehension score of at least 75 percent and the ability to use experiences that are pertinent to the reading selection. It is also important that the teacher informally observe the student's ability to use vocabulary and language structure in his oral discussion that is as complex as that used in the reading selection.

## Administering and Scoring the Basic Reading Inventory

Since the Basic Reading Inventory is an informal test, there is no particular set of procedures that must be rigidly followed. The teacher, nevertheless, must thoroughly familiarize herself with the recommended procedures for giving the test *before* asking a student to read the graded word lists and graded passages.

Before the teacher can administer the Basic Reading Inventory, she should have some general idea of the student's reading ability. There are several ways the teacher can gather information for making this decision. She can consult the cumulative record from the previous year to note the level at which the student was reading. The teacher can also use her judgment based upon the student's reading performance in her classroom. Regardless of the methods used to decide where to begin administration of the reading inventory, it is important that the student experience success with the initial graded word lists and graded passages. The teacher should, therefore, begin where the student is very likely to find the material easy. The procedure for actually administering and scoring the reading inventory may be divided into seven major sections.

## 1. Establishing Rapport

If the reading inventory is to yield valid and reliable results, it is necessary to obtain the student's cooperation. In an effort to establish rapport, the teacher may wish to give the student some idea about how his reading will be evaluated. The teacher may also want to explore the student's interests and answer his questions about the testing. This may reduce the anxiety that often accompanies a testing situation. Teachers should carefully note that rapport is not always fully established before the administration of a reading inventory actually begins. In some cases, rapport is steadily increased throughout the testing situation. In other cases, interaction between the teacher and the student may become strained during the testing. If this occurs, the teacher should attempt to establish rapport once again.

During the early stages of establishing rapport, as well as throughout the administration of the reading inventory, the experienced teacher has the opportunity to gain valuable diagnostic information in several areas. She can appraise the student's oral language facility through informal conversation and observe how well the student responds to specific questions that are asked after he reads the graded passages. The experienced teacher may also gain insight into how the student approaches the reading task, his attitude toward himself and reading, and how he attempts to unlock or decode unknown words. The teacher can also ask specific questions such as "What is reading?" and "What do you do when you read?" to gain insight into how the student views the reading process. When the teacher feels that adequate rapport has been established, it is generally advisable to begin the reading inventory with the graded word lists.

## 2. Administering, Scoring, and Determining Reading Levels from the Graded Word Lists

There are four purposes for giving the graded word lists. First, the word lists will provide the approximate level at which the student should begin reading the graded paragraphs. Second, the teacher can obtain a general idea of the student's three reading levels. Third, the teacher will be able to study the student's word analysis skills. Fourth, she can get some idea of the extent of the student's sight vocabulary. Since the word lists are not a natural reading situation, extreme caution should guide the teacher. The word lists do not assess the student's ability to comprehend and are, therefore, an inappropriate measure of a student's reading ability. Goodman (1965) has demonstrated that students decode much more readily when words appear in context than when they appear in lists. Also, Marzano and others (1978) have cautioned teachers about basing assessment solely on a word recognition test.

To administer the graded word lists, the teacher will need the word lists for the student and the performance booklet in which she will record the student's responses. The recommended procedure for administering the graded word lists is to present the student with a list of words and ask him to pronounce them rapidly. As the student reads down each list of words, the teacher records his responses in a performance booklet. The word list the teacher initially selects should, if at all possible, be very easy for the student.

An alternative method for administering the graded word lists is to copy the words onto individual 3″ by 5″ cards. Individual cards allow uniform exposure time to all words. Each word should be presented for no more than one second. This procedure clearly establishes a timed and untimed condition for each word. Specific instructions for using this procedure are discussed by Jacobs and Searfoss (1979).

The teacher derives two scores for each graded word list administered to the student (see Table 2). One score represents the student's immediate responses to the words and is called the *timed presentation*. The second score represents the student's correction of the words missed during the timed presentation. The opportunity for the student to study each word missed in an attempt to pronounce it is called the *untimed* or *analysis score*. If the student does not know or mispronounces any words on the first attempt (i.e., on the timed presentation), the teacher returns to each of these words after the student has finished the list and gives him an opportunity to analyze the word in an attempt to arrive at its correct pronunciation. The student's *immediate* responses are recorded by the teacher in the timed response column. The responses the student makes when the teacher gives him an opportunity to study the words missed are recorded in the untimed column.

It is very important that the teacher promptly record the student's responses because any delays are likely to result in incorrect reporting. The use of a tape recorder may prove quite helpful for the teacher. The graded word lists are generally continued until the student is no longer able to achieve a total score of at least fourteen correct words on the untimed test or when the situation becomes frustrating for the student. Teacher judgment should help determine when to stop the test.

In an effort to exemplify the scoring of graded word lists, the reader is directed to Table 2 which contains Jeff's performance on the pre-primer and primer word lists. An empty space next to a word means that Jeff pronounced it correctly. Miscues in word recognition are noted as follows: "DK" indicates that he said "I don't know." Single letters or phonetic symbols represent Jeff's attempt to pronounce the word. The plus (+) indicates that he corrected a miscalled word. When Jeff said a word which was different from the stimulus word, it is noted in the appropriate column. Other pertinent comments that might have diagnostic significance (e.g., skips unknown words; uses phonic knowledge) are also noted by the teacher.

**Table 2**
Example of Jeff's Performance on Two Graded Word Lists

| List A-A | Timed | Untimed | List A | Timed | Untimed |
|---|---|---|---|---|---|
| 1. and | | | 1. ask | *as* | + |
| 2. blue | *O.K.* | + | 2. bad | | |
| 3. let | *law* | + | 3. face | | |
| 4. tree | | | 4. something | | |
| 5. go | | | 5. went | | |
| 6. my | *me* | + | 6. laughed | *lā* | *laugh* |
| 7. at | | | 7. birthday | | |
| 8. look | | | 8. new | | |
| 9. up | | | 9. his | | |
| 10. red | | | 10. reads | *rēad* | + |
| 11. for | | | 11. wagon | | |
| 12. the | | | 12. but | *bad* | *bed* |
| 13. if | | | 13. soon | | |
| 14. where | | | 14. they | | |
| 15. bed | | | 15. eat | | |
| 16. very | | | 16. matter | | |
| 17. here | | | 17. train | | |
| 18. that | | | 18. into | *in* | + |
| 19. is | | | 19. white | | |
| 20. what | *when* | *when* | 20. children | | |
| Number Correct | 16 | 3 | Number Correct | 15 | 3 |
| Total Score | | 19 | Total Score | | 18 |

**Scoring Guide for Graded Word Lists**

| Independent | Instructional | Frustration |
|---|---|---|
| 20 19 | 18 17 16 15 14 | 13 or less |

Jeff's scores are shown at the bottom of each column of words. For the pre-primer (A-A) word list, the score of 16 indicates that he correctly pronounced 16 of the 20 words on the timed presentation. The four words not correctly pronounced on the timed presentation were numbers 2, 3, 6, and 20. From his score on the *untimed* column, the teacher can note that Jeff corrected three of his initial miscues (numbers 2, 3, and 6), thereby achieving a total score of 19 correct words. At the primer level Jeff achieved a score of 15 on the timed presentation and a total score of 18 because he corrected three (numbers 1, 10, and 18) of his initial miscues.

The teacher can use the total number of words the student correctly pronounces on each graded word list for a general idea of his reading levels. To convert total scores to a rough estimate of the various reading levels, the teacher should compare the total number of correct words for each list of words to the general criteria in Table 3 or the scoring guide at the bottom of the word lists. From Table 2 the teacher can note that Jeff achieved a total score of 19 correct words on the pre-primer list. According to Table 3 or the scoring guide below the word lists, a score of 19 would indicate an independent level. The total score of 18 for the primer graded word list converts to the instructional level. From the results reported thus far, it is not possible to approximate Jeff's frustration level. The teacher would need to continue the testing until he mispronounced seven words or appeared to be having considerable difficulty. When this point is reached, the teacher would proceed to the graded passages. Remember, however, that reading levels estimated in this manner represent very rough indications of reading ability. The inadequacies of graded word lists are recognized by teachers who know that some students can identify words in isolation that cause difficulty in meaningful reading material. Other students who have difficulty with words in isolation can identify words in meaningful reading material. It is important, therefore, to recognize the limitations of graded word lists.

**Table 3**
General Criteria for Reading Levels: Words in Isolation

| Levels | Total Score on Word List |
|---|---|
| Independent | 19–20 |
| Instructional | 14–18 |
| Frustration | 13 or less |

From the example presented in Table 2, it was noted that Jeff achieved a total score of 19 on the pre-primer list and a score of 18 on the primer list. These scores should then be entered in a summary chart similar to that shown in Table 4. To determine the reading levels corresponding to these two scores, consult Table 3 or the scoring guide at the bottom of the word lists. According to the criteria, Jeff achieved an independent level on the pre-primer word list and an instructional level on the primer word list.

The teacher should check her understanding of this procedure by attempting to find the reading levels that correspond to Jeff's performance on the first and second grade word lists as noted in Table 4. This task can be accomplished by taking the score given in Table 4 for the first grade word list (15) and finding the corresponding reading level from Table 3. The reading level should then be entered next to the number of words correct. This procedure can be repeated for the score on the second grade word list.

**Table 4**
Summary Sheet for Jeff's Performance on the
Basic Reading Inventory

| Grade | Word Recognition | | | | Comprehension | | | | | |
|---|---|---|---|---|---|---|---|---|---|---|
| | Isolation | | Context | | Oral Reading Form Ⓐ B C | | | Silent Reading Form A B C | | |
| | Total Score | Level | Percent Correct | Level | Percent Correct | Level | | Percent Correct | Level | Rate |
| PP | 19 | Ind. | 100 | | 100 | | | | | |
| P | 18 | Inst. | 99 | | 90 | | | | | |
| 1 | 15 | | 95 | | 80 | | | | | |
| 2 | 12 | | 88 | | 50 | | | | | |
| 3 | | | | | | | | | | |

## 3. Administering the Graded Passages

Prior to actually administering the graded passages, the teacher must develop some system for recording the student's responses. There are numerous systems and techniques for coding reading miscues (Goodman and Burke, 1972; Johnson and Kress, 1965; Pflaum, 1979). Table 5 contains a suggested method for recording miscues in oral reading. The reader should carefully study and learn the suggested procedure so that it can be used and referred to later when actual examples of a student's oral reading are considered.

It is generally a wise procedure to begin administering the graded passages at least one level below the student's highest independent level on the graded word lists. If a student, for example, achieved independent levels on the word lists for the pre-primer, primer, first, and second grade levels, it is recommended that the teacher begin the graded passages at the first grade level. If the passage is too difficult for the student, it is permissible for the teacher to give the student the next lower level and go as low as necessary to find the level where the student can read fluently with excellent comprehension.

Once the starting level for reading the graded passages is determined, the general procedure on each successive passage is the same. The teacher may wish to establish a definite purpose for reading each passage. She may also tell the student to think about the passage since he will be asked some questions about the passage he reads. (Remind him that he should do the best he can with hard words. The teacher can gain insights about the student's word recognition strategies by not pronouncing unknown words for him. Occasionally, some students may need to be told a word if they pause for ten or fifteen seconds; however, the recommended procedure is to allow students to read the graded passages using their strategies for

*SUBSTITUTIONS*

*a*

Jim saw the boy.

*OMISSIONS*

Poor little (Baby) Bear could not move from the tall tree.

*INSERTIONS*

*he*

He strolled along the path and soon^was deep in the forest.

*REVERSALS*

(Are they twins?

*REPETITIONS*

A. Correcting a miscue

*@*   *see*

Baby Bear did not know where he was.

B. Abandoning a correct form

*@c*  *along*

He stayed alone in the pine tree all night.

C. Unsuccessfully attempting to correct

*@c*  *2. ha-*
      *1. heavy*

He had slept hard all night.

*ADDITIONAL MARKINGS*

A. Partial words

*res—*

The hunters saw the shooting arrows and rescued the boys.

B. Non-word substitutions

*$ frontmer*

Men on the frontier often had shooting contests.

C. Dialect

*@ goed*

He went home.

D. Intonation

*/*

He played a record that was his favorite.

pronouncing words.) The student is then asked to read the passage orally at sight. While the student is reading from the graded passage, the teacher uses a performance booklet to keep a careful record of the exact way in which the student reads the passage. The suggested method for recording a student's oral reading, presented in Table 5, should be a valuable aid to the teacher or prospective teacher who has not yet developed her own system for recording. The teacher should remember that she is *testing* the student, not teaching him. She should not, therefore, try to teach the student how to unlock a particular word. Her major task is to record the manner in which the student reads the passage by noting omissions, repetitions, substitutions, and other miscues.

After the student finishes reading the passage, the teacher asks the comprehension questions. The student should not refer to the passage when answering the questions. In addition, the teacher should not help the student arrive at the correct answers to the questions. If a comprehension question is answered incorrectly, the teacher should merely note the student's response and go on to the next question. The teacher may, however, ask for clarification if the answer for a particular question is not clear. The student's answers to the comprehension questions need not conform exactly to the answers in the performance booklets; responses similar in meaning to the printed answer should be scored as correct. Recording the student's verbatim responses to the comprehension questions will make it much easier for the teacher to score the comprehension questions. This general procedure is continued with subsequent passages until the student is unable to answer satisfactorily at least half of the comprehension questions and/or has approximately ten or more significant word recognition miscues.

Table 6 contains Jeff's oral reading performance on a second grade passage. The notations indicate that he substituted *Bob* for *Bill, so* for *soon,* and *was* for *saw.* All three of the substitutions, however, were corrected. He also substituted *minute* for *moment* and *a* for *the* and did not correct these two miscues, possibly because they did not result in significant changes in the meaning of the selection. Jeff also inserted *trees,* but again, the meaning was not altered. The selection was read with good fluency and phrasing.

On the 10 comprehension questions Jeff responded freely and demonstrated the ability to answer various types of questions. (The + indicates correct responses; underlining indicates student's responses.) Jeff apparently forgot the name of one kind of leaf Bill found in the woods (hence he received half credit); nevertheless, his understanding of the passage was excellent. From the general criteria for the three reading levels, it would appear that this passage is at Jeff's independent level since he made no significant miscues and had excellent comprehension (95 percent).

Once a teacher becomes familiar with the graded passages, it is possible to use a retelling strategy to assess comprehension. In a retelling strategy, the teacher invites the student to tell about the passage that has just been read. The teacher may ask specific questions; however, she should not give the student information that has not already been mentioned. Using Jeff's reading of the second grade passage in Table 6 for illustration, the teacher would first ask him to tell about what he read. Suppose Jeff said that the passage is about a boy who went to camp for the first time. The teacher could encourage the student to relate further events. She could also ask him to give the boy's name. Through experience, the teacher will gain confidence in her ability to extract the main ideas and important details in the passages without asking the comprehension questions.

## Table 6
### Example of Jeff's Performance on a Graded Passage

It was the first time ⓒ *Bob* |Bill went to camp. He was very happy to be there. ⓒ *So* |Soon he went for a walk in the woods to look for many kinds of leaves. He found leaves from some maple^*trees* and oak trees. As Bill walked in the woods, he ⓒ *was* |saw some animal tracks. At that *minute* moment, a mouse ran into a small hole by a tree. Bill wondered if the tracks were made by *a* the mouse. He looked around for other animals. He did not see any. The only thing Bill saw was an old bird's nest in a pine tree.

*good phrasing and intonation*

M　1. _+_　What is this story about?
　　　　　(a boy at camp)
　　　　　*Bill at camp*

F　2. _+_　Why did Bill go walking in the woods?
　　　　　(to look for leaves)

F　3. _+_　Did Bill enjoy going to camp? How do you know?
　　　　　(yes, the story said he was happy there)

F　4. _½_　What kinds of leaves did Bill find in the woods?
　　　　　(maple and oak leaves)
　　　　　*what other kinds? I don't know.*

F　5. _+_　Where did the mouse go?
　　　　　(into a small hole by a tree)

F　6. _+_　What else did Bill see besides the mouse?
　　　　　(a bird's nest and animal tracks)

I　7. _+_　Do you think Bill went on this walk by himself? What makes you think so?
　　　　　(any logical response)
　　　　　*Yes, he didn't talk to another person.*

I　8. _+_　Why do you think Bill was happy at camp?
　　　　　(any logical response)
　　　　　*he liked to be there*

E　9. _+_　Do you think it is important for boys and girls to go to camp?
　　　　　(any logical response)
　　　　　*Yes, you learn about nature*

V　10. _+_　What are "tracks"?
　　　　　(footprints made in the dirt; something made by animals when they walk or run)

### Scoring Guide: Two

Percent of Word Recognition in Context

| 100 99 | 98 97 96 | 95 | 94 93 92 91 | 90 or less |
|---|---|---|---|---|
| Independent Level | Independent or Instructional | Instructional Level | Instructional or Frustration | Frustration Level |
| 100 95 90 | 85 80 | 75 | 70 65 60 55 | 50 or less |

Percent of Comprehension

In actual practice, many teachers feel more comfortable in combining the retelling strategy with some of the comprehension questions. This procedure permits the teacher to maintain the necessary flexibility to gather the information needed to make an accurate assessment of the student's understanding of the passage. Also, as the teacher moves toward a retelling strategy, she will see that a number of the comprehension questions are not essential for judging the student's comprehension of a given passage. A few of the comprehension questions in the passages can be answered from the student's previous knowledge (especially the vocabulary [V] and evaluation [E] questions). Although the retelling strategy is more subjective in its scoring, the purpose in assessing comprehension is to determine whether the passage is at the student's independent, instructional, or frustration level. If the teacher keeps this purpose in mind, the end result should be satisfactory. Goodman and Burke (1972) have offered additional suggestions to teachers who are interested in gaining proficiency in using a retelling strategy to assess the student's understanding of his reading.

## 4. Determining Reading Levels from the Word Recognition in Context Score

The teacher can determine whether the passage is at a student's independent, instructional, or frustration level by considering: (1) the competence with which the student reads; and (2) the student's behavior while reading. In order to determine the accuracy with which the student reads the passage, the teacher must determine the student's word recognition score. The word recognition score is found by determining the percentage of *significant* miscues the student makes during his oral reading of the graded passages. Since all the passages contain 50 or 100 words, the percentage can be determined quite easily.

The notion of what constitutes a significant miscue differs among reading authorities. Some reading authorities maintain that only substitutions, insertions, and requests for teacher aid should be counted in computing the word recognition score for passage reading (Johnson and Kress, 1965). More recent evidence (Allen and Watson, 1976; Goodman, 1972; Lipton, 1972; Recht, 1976) seems to suggest that certain substitutions, insertions, omissions, and the like do not seriously damage the student's understanding of the passage; hence, such miscues should not be held against him.

> It must be remembered that accurate recognition is not the major objective in reading. *The goal is always meaning.* Because even proficient readers make errors on unfamiliar material, teachers must resist the temptation to meticulously correct all inconsequential mistakes. They must always ask whether a particular miscue really makes a difference (Goodman, 1971, p. 14).

It would appear that the best advice to give teachers and prospective teachers for counting significant miscues is to include those omissions, insertions, substitutions, and other miscues that appear to affect comprehension. The following method is suggested:

1. Count the total number of miscues in the passage.
2. Find the total of all dialect miscues, all corrected miscues, and all miscues that do not change the meaning.

3. Subtract this total from the total number of miscues. The result is the number of significant miscues.

In short, significant miscues affect meaning.

From Jeff's oral reading of a second grade passage (Table 6, p. 16), it is readily apparent that he made numerous miscues. Although none of the miscues appears to affect the meaning of the passage, the teacher decided to lump all the miscues together as *one* significant miscue. To determine Jeff's percent of word recognition, the teacher can merely subtract 1 from 100, thereby achieving a score of 99 percent. The word recognition in context score is circled in the scoring guide and written on the summary sheet of the performance booklet.

The same procedure is used to determine the percentage of word recognition for the other graded passages at and above the primer level. Since the pre-primer selections contain 50 words, the teacher would count each significant miscue as 2 percentage points and then subtract from 100.

After the percentage indicating the accuracy of word recognition in context is determined, the teacher should enter the score on a summary sheet of the performance booklet. The teacher should then consult Table 7 or the scoring guide below each passage, either of which will yield the reading levels that correspond to the various percentages for words in context. For example, a student who attains 99 percent accuracy for words in context would achieve an independent level for that passage. When the student's percentages differ from the criteria presented in Table 7, teacher judgment must be used. The gray areas on the scoring guide indicate when teacher judgment is necessary. This judgment, however, should be held in abeyance until the scores for comprehension are determined. The recommended procedure is to write *Ind./Inst.* on the summary sheet when the percentages are between 95 and 99. When the percentages are between 90 and 95, enter *Inst./Frust.* on the summary sheet. Table 4 (p. 13) contains various sample percentages. By consulting Table 7 or the scoring guide, the teacher should determine the reading levels that correspond to the various percentages and place the appropriate levels in Table 4 (p. 13).

**Table 7**
General Criteria for Reading Levels: Words in Context

| Levels | Percent of Words Correct |
| --- | --- |
| Independent | 99 |
| Instructional | 95 |
| Frustration | 90 |

## 5. Determining Reading Levels from the Comprehension Questions

The comprehension score is the percentage of questions answered correctly. It is derived by dividing the number of correct responses by the total number of questions. If a student, for example, answers 5 of 10 comprehension questions correctly, he would achieve a comprehension score of 50 percent. To convert this percentage into one of the three reading levels, the teacher would merely consult Table 8 or the

**Table 8**
General Criteria for Reading Levels: Comprehension

| Levels | Percent of Questions Answered Correctly |
|---|---|
| Independent | 90 |
| Instructional | 75 |
| Frustration | 50 |

scoring guide. A score of 50 percent indicates that the passage is at the student's frustration level.

The above procedure, however, is not directly applicable to the pre-primer passages because they contain only 5 questions; hence, each question counts 20 percent. Teacher judgment must be exercised in determining the student's comprehension score. A student could miss one question at the pre-primer level (a comprehension score of 80 percent) and one question at the primer level (a comprehension score of 90 percent). If the teacher decided that the score from the pre-primer level did not accurately reflect the student's achievement, it would be permissible for the teacher to place more emphasis on the score at the primer level when summarizing the results of all passages administered.

Table 4 contains Jeff's percentage scores for the comprehension questions in the pre-primer through second grade levels. The teacher, by consulting Table 8 or the scoring guide below each passage, should determine the reading level that corresponds to each graded passage and place these levels in Table 4 (p. 13). When a student's percentages differ from the criteria presented in Table 8, teacher judgment must be used. The recommended procedure when the percentages are 80 or 85 is to record *Ind./Inst.* on the summary sheet. Percentages of 55, 60, 65, or 70 should be recorded as *Inst./Frust.* on the summary sheet. The scoring guide clearly indicates gray areas that require teacher judgment. The determination of reading levels that require teacher judgment is discussed in the section on Assimilating Results (p. 23).

Teachers who choose to use the retelling strategy to assess comprehension may: (1) determine a percent score from the student's retelling; or (2) identify the passage as one of the three reading levels without noting a specific percent of comprehension. The main point to be kept in mind is whether the student's comprehension of the passage is at the independent, instructional, or frustration level.

## 6. Determining Reading Levels and Rate from Silent Reading

If the teacher decides to have a student read silently, she should use the passages from a different form of the Basic Reading Inventory. It is recommended that the teacher begin with a reading passage that is at the student's independent level. As the student reads the passage silently, the teacher times the student's reading and notes behavioral characteristics such as lip movement, finger pointing, etc. After silent reading, the student's comprehension is assessed. Comprehension can be evaluated with the retelling strategy or by asking the comprehension questions. The student continues to read increasingly difficult passages until his frustration level is determined. The various percentages and corresponding reading levels should be entered at the appropriate place on the summary sheet. These silent reading levels can be used in conjunction with the student's oral reading performance to arrive at his three reading levels.

A formula for determining a student's rate of reading is provided on each graded-passage page in the performance booklet. The 6000 for each graded passage above the pre-primer level was arrived at by multiplying the number of words per selection (approximately 100) by sixty. The teacher who wants to determine a student's rate of reading can do so by using the formula. The teacher should record as the divisor of the formula the time (in seconds) the student takes to read the passage. Perform the necessary division, and the resulting numeral will be a rough estimate of the student's rate in words per minute (WPM). For example, suppose a middle-grade student took 70 seconds to read a fourth grade selection. The teacher would divide 6000 by 70. The result is a reading rate of approximately 86 words per minute (WPM).

$$
\begin{array}{r}
85.7 \text{ WPM} \\
70\overline{)6000} \\
\underline{560} \\
400 \\
\underline{350} \\
500 \\
\underline{490}
\end{array}
$$

Taylor, Frackenpohl, and Pettee (1960) have provided some norms for silent reading rate (see Table 9). It should be remembered that reading rate can vary greatly according to the material being read, the student's interest in the material, and the purpose for which it is being read. These norms, when used by teachers, should be considered very rough approximations.

**Table 9**
Norms for Silent Reading Rate

| | Grade | | | | | | | |
|---|---|---|---|---|---|---|---|---|
| | 1 | 2 | 3 | 4 | 5 | 6 | 7 | 8 |
| Rate with 70% Comprehension | 80* | 115 | 138 | 158 | 173 | 185 | 195 | 204 |

*Expressed in words per minute (WPM).

## 7. Determining the Listening Level

In addition to the three reading levels, the teacher may wish to get a rough estimate of the student's listening level or potential for substantial growth in reading. Intelligence tests are sometimes used to estimate potential for reading; however, their limitations have led some teachers to read graded passages to a student and determine the highest level of material that the student can understand. Undertaking such a procedure is known as determining the student's listening level.

The listening level is determined by the *teacher* reading increasingly difficult passages to the student. After each passage is read *to* the student, the teacher asks the student comprehension questions. The criteria for estimating the student's listening level is a comprehension score of at least 75 percent. The teacher should also informally note the student's ability to use vocabulary and language structure as complex as that used in the passage read.

It is recommended that the teacher begin reading a passage that is at least one year below the student's instructional level. The teacher should then continue reading more difficult passages until the student is unable to achieve a score of at least 75 percent on the comprehension questions. The *highest* passage at which the student achieves a score of at least 75 percent is his listening level.

Suppose, for example, that Tom's instructional level is second grade for oral and silent reading and the teacher wishes to determine his listening level or potential. She should choose a passage at the first grade level from a form of the Basic Reading Inventory that he has not read orally or silently. After she reads the passage, Tom responds to the comprehension questions. If he achieves a score of 75 percent or greater, the teacher continues reading increasingly difficult passages until he is unable to obtain a comprehension score of at least 75 percent. The highest level at which Tom obtains a score of at least 75 percent is identified as his capacity level. To illustrate this procedure, consider Tom's data in Table 10.

### Table 10
#### Data for Tom's Listening Level

| Level of Passage | Comprehension Percentage |
|---|---|
| 1 (C 1417) | 90 |
| 2 (C 8224) | 100 |
| 3 (C 3183) | 80 |
| 4 (C 5414) | 60 |

Based on these data, Tom's listening level would be third grade since that was the highest level at which he achieved a comprehension score of at least 75 percent. Since his listening level (third grade) is higher than his instructional level (second grade), the teacher has reason to believe that Tom has the potential to increase his reading ability. In this instance, listening comprehension can be viewed as a favorable prognostic sign; namely, the student should be able to understand material at the third grade level once he acquires the necessary reading competence.

There are, of course, some limitations for using the listening level as an indicator of reading potential. Limitations within the assessment process as well as a student's auditory handicaps and/or unfamiliarity with standard English reduce the importance that the teacher should attach to a listening level. In addition, bright students in the middle and upper grades may have reading abilities that exceed their listening abilities. For these and other reasons, teachers should consider the listening level as a rough estimate of reading potential that needs to be supported from the results of other measures of intellectual capacity.

## SUMMARY OF ADMINISTRATION
## AND SCORING PROCEDURES

To determine a student's independent, instructional, and frustration levels, administer the three reading tests included in the Basic Reading Inventory as follows:

**WORD RECOGNITION IN ISOLATION:** Select a graded word list at a reading level that will be easy for the student. Ask the student to pronounce the words rapidly. Record the student's responses in the timed column beside the corresponding word list in the performance booklet.

Return to mispronounced or unknown words for a second attempt at analysis, and note the student's responses in the untimed column. Administer successive word lists until the student is no longer able to achieve a total score of at least fourteen correct words or until the student becomes frustrated.

**Scoring:** Total the correct responses in the timed and untimed columns. Consult the criteria on the general scoring guide shown below to determine the reading level achieved on each graded word list. Record the number-correct scores and the reading levels on the summary sheet of the performance booklet.

**WORD RECOGNITION IN CONTEXT:** Ask the student to read aloud the passage graded one level *below* the highest independent level achieved on the graded word lists. As the student reads the passage, record all miscues such as omissions, repetitions, substitutions, etc. on the corresponding copy of the passage found in the performance booklet.

**Scoring:** To find the percent-correct score, count the number of significant miscues (those that affect meaning) in each graded passage. At the pre-primer level, each significant miscue is valued at 2 percentage points and subtracted from 100. At the primer level and above, each significant miscue is valued at 1 percentage point and subtracted from 100.

To determine reading levels from the percent-correct scores, consult the criteria on the general scoring guide shown below. Record the percent-correct scores and the reading levels on the summary sheet of the performance booklet.

**COMPREHENSION:** Ask the comprehension questions that are beside the passage in the performance booklet and record the student's responses. Continue administering graded passages until the student has ten or more significant word recognition miscues, is unable to answer half the comprehension questions, or demonstrates behavior associated with frustration.

**Scoring:** To find the percent-correct score achieved on each passage, divide the number of correct responses by the number of questions.

To convert the percent-correct scores into reading levels, consult the criteria on the general scoring guide below. (Teacher judgment must be exercised at the pre-primer level because the limited number of questions may not permit precise measurement of achievement.) Record the percent-correct scores and the reading levels on the summary sheet of the performance booklet.

### General Scoring Guide for Reading Levels

| Subtest of Basic Reading Inventory | Independent Level | Independent or Instructional Level | Instructional Level | Instructional or Frustration Level | Frustration Level |
|---|---|---|---|---|---|
| Word Recognition in Isolation | 20–19 | | 18–14 | | 13 or less |
| Word Recognition in Context (%) | 99 | 98–96 | 95 | 94–91 | 90 or less |
| Comprehension (%) | 90 | 85–80 | 75 | 70–55 | 50 or less |

Note: Teacher judgment is necessary in gray areas.

# Assimilating the Results from the Basic Reading Inventory

Once the teacher has used Table 4 to summarize the test results for the graded word lists, the words in context, and passage comprehension, she can determine the student's independent level, instructional level, and frustration level. Table 11 contains a summary of Jeff's performance on the Basic Reading Inventory. The various percentages and levels should correspond to the teacher's efforts to complete the examples that were presented in Table 4 (p. 13). The teacher should check her results with Table 11 and resolve any discrepancies.

**Table 11**

Summary of Jeff's Performance on Form A
of the Basic Reading Inventory

| Grade | Word Recognition | | | | Comprehension | | | | |
|---|---|---|---|---|---|---|---|---|---|
| | Isolation | | Context | | Oral Reading Form Ⓐ B C | | Silent Reading Form A B C | | |
| | Total Score | Level | Percent Correct | Level | Percent Correct | Level | Percent Correct | Level | Rate |
| PP | 19 | Ind. | 100 | Ind. | 100 | Ind. | | | |
| P | 18 | Inst. | 99 | Ind. | 90 | Ind. | | | |
| 1 | 15 | Inst. | 95 | Inst. | 80 | Inst. | | | |
| 2 | 12 | Frust. | 88 | Frust. | 50 | Frust. | | | |
| 3 | | | | | | | | | |

From the data presented in Tables 4 and 11, it would appear that Jeff's independent levels are pre-primer and primer. Since the independent level is the *highest* level at which a student can read books by himself, the primer level would be his independent level. Materials at the first grade level of difficulty should provide the basis for instruction; hence, it is his instructional level. At this level the student should make maximum progress under teacher guidance. The second grade level, according to the criteria, appears to be this student's frustration level. He should not, therefore, be asked to read material at this level. In summary, Jeff's three reading levels are: independent—primer, instructional—first grade, and frustration—second grade.

It should be noted that most summary sheets, unlike Table 11, will not provide the teacher with such clear distinctions among the three reading levels. When discrepancies arise, the teacher must use her judgment in determining the student's three levels. Frequently, it is wise to consider the student's performance *preceding* and *following* the level in question, as well as his performance *within* a particular passage. Interpreting the summary of Bob's reading, presented in Table 12, requires some teacher judgment.

**Table 12**
Summary of Bob's Performance on Form B
of the Basic Reading Inventory

| Grade | Word Recognition | | | | Comprehension | | | | |
| --- | --- | --- | --- | --- | --- | --- | --- | --- | --- |
| | Isolation | | Context | | Oral Reading Form A Ⓑ C | | Silent Reading Form A B C | | |
| | Total Score | Level | Percent Correct | Level | Percent Correct | Level | Percent Correct | Level | Rate |
| 1 | 20 | Ind. | 99 | Ind. | 90 | Ind. | | | |
| 2 | 20 | Ind. | 96 | Ind/Inst. | 90 | Ind. | | | |
| 3 | 15 | Inst. | 95 | Inst. | 75 | Inst. | | | |
| 4 | 11 | Frust. | 95 | Inst. | 40 | Frust. | | | |
| 5 | | | | | | | | | |

The scores for the first and third grade levels present no problems since the numerals correspond to those given in Tables 3, 7, and 8. At the second grade level, however, word recognition in context is below the criteria in Table 7 for independent level. Since Bob's other two scores at the second grade level are marked *independent,* the teacher may conclude that his reading is at the independent level. For the fourth grade level, Bob achieved instructional level for word recognition in context; however, his scores for word recognition in isolation and comprehension are at the frustration level. Since Bob is unable to comprehend the material satisfactorily, the teacher should regard fourth grade as his frustration level. Now, by analyzing Bob's performance *within* a given graded passage and *between* the four graded passages, the teacher may verify earlier judgments and conclude that his three reading levels are: independent—second grade, instructional—third grade, and frustration—fourth grade. Teachers should also note that it is possible for some students to have a range of several grades within the instructional level. If, for example, Bob's scores in Table 12 were changed so that the comprehension score at the second grade level was 80 percent, the three reading levels would probably be: independent—first grade, instructional—second grade and third grade, and frustration—fourth grade.

Another summary sheet that requires teacher judgment is shown in Table 13. Study the percentages and make a judgment with regard to Hank's independent, instructional, and frustration levels before continuing.

At the fourth grade level the teacher must resolve the word recognition score in context. A score of 98 percent could be either independent or instructional; however, by examining the other scores *within* that level, the teacher should judge fourth grade as an independent level. The fifth grade level requires judgment in comprehension. Since the 85 percent score in comprehension is near the independent level (90 percent is "required") and the other two scores within this level are independent, the teacher should conclude that the fifth grade level is also independent. At the sixth grade level the 97 percent in word recognition in context is best identified as instructional since Hank's other two scores are instructional.

**Table 13**
Summary of Hank's Performance on Form C
of the Basic Reading Inventory

| Grade | Word Recognition | | | | Comprehension | | | |
| | Isolation | | Context | | Oral Reading Form A B Ⓒ | | Silent Reading Form A B C | | |
| | Total Score | Level | Percent Correct | Level | Percent Correct | Level | Percent Correct | Level | Rate |
|---|---|---|---|---|---|---|---|---|---|
| 4 | 20 | Ind. | 98 | Ind./Inst | 100 | Ind. | | | |
| 5 | 19 | Ind. | 99 | Ind. | 85 | Ind./Inst. | | | |
| 6 | 18 | Inst. | 97 | Ind./Inst. | 75 | Inst. | | | |
| 7 | 15 | Inst. | 93 | Inst./Frust. | 55 | Inst./Frust. | | | |
| 8 | 14 | Inst./Frust. | 90 | Frust. | 40 | Frust. | | | |

The seventh grade level requires teacher judgment in two areas: word recognition in context and comprehension. Both of these scores appear to be nearer the frustration level, so a tentative judgment for the seventh grade level is frustration.

Although some judgment is required at the eighth grade level, the words in isolation score is near frustration and the other two scores are clearly frustration. The teacher must now decide on Hank's reading levels. From the earlier judgments, his three reading levels would probably be: independent—fifth grade, instructional— sixth grade, and frustration—seventh grade. Although Hank is quite good at pronouncing words at the seventh grade level, the teacher placed considerable emphasis on his comprehension. Generally, the recommended procedure is to place greater emphasis on comprehension. **Remember that the goal of reading is reconstructing meaning from print.** The ability to pronounce words *is* important; nevertheless, word recognition ability must always be judged with regard to the student's ability to understand the selection. To help teachers make decisions, **place emphasis first on comprehension** (both oral and silent), then word recognition in *context,* and finally word recognition in *isolation.*

It is also important to take the behavioral characteristics for each reading level into consideration to aid in the proper placement of students. A student, for example, may have percentages high enough to read independently at a certain level of difficulty; however, he may appear to be quite nervous and exhibit behavioral characteristics which lead the teacher to conclude that such a level is too difficult for independent reading. It would seem prudent for teachers to exercise extreme care in determining a student's three reading levels. It is always easier to move a student to a higher level if he finds the material too easy than to initially place him in a book which might be difficult and frustrating.

In most cases the three reading levels serve as a starting point for effective reading instruction. Since the reading levels are determined in a relatively short period of time, they may not be entirely accurate. The teacher should not, therefore, consider a student's three reading levels to be rigid and static. If, in working with the student, the teacher finds that his various reading levels are not accurate, she should make the necessary adjustments.

# Using the Basic Reading Inventory to Enhance Instruction

In addition to using the Basic Reading Inventory to estimate a student's three reading levels, the results can also be used to determine tentative strengths and weaknesses in reading. Several strategies are suggested for both word attack and comprehension.

## Determining Strengths and Weaknesses in Word Attack

*Strategy 1: Simple Error Analysis.* The teacher can devise a method for analyzing the miscues made during oral reading in an effort to find patterns. These patterns may indicate certain strengths and weaknesses in word attack. By recording a student's miscues from the reading inventory on a sheet similar to that in Table 14, the teacher may make hypotheses about a student's needs in reading. Suppose, for example, that Sam's errors from the word recognition tests and oral reading passages revealed the information contained in Table 14. Based on these data, it would appear that Sam is able to apply the initial sounds in those words he has difficulty pro-

### Table 14
Summary of Sam's Oral Reading Performance

| SUBSTITUTIONS | | | |
|---|---|---|---|
| **Different Beginnings** | **Different Middles** | **Different Endings** | **Different in Several Parts** |
| | ran for rain<br>naw - now<br>well - will<br>walk - work<br>barn - burn | fly - flew<br>had - have<br>big - bigger | a for the<br>road - street<br>in - into<br>big - huge |

| **Insertions** | **Omissions** | **Repetitions** | **Miscellaneous** |
|---|---|---|---|
| big<br>always | she<br>spiders<br>many | /// | |

nouncing. He has considerable difficulty, however, with the middle of words. Upon further analysis of his medial errors, it would seem that a lack of vowel knowledge may be contributing to his difficulties in word recognition. It is also evident that many of these miscues are substitutions that probably distort the meaning of the reading selection. Sam may profit from situation 5 in Appendix B. Sam has also made several other substitutions; however, these substitutions (*a* for *the; road* for *street*, etc.) do not result in significant changes in the meaning of the passage and do not require any instruction. The repetitions Sam made may indicate a problem that requires the attention of the teacher or an effective reading strategy. Teachers should evaluate such repetitions within the context of situation 1 in Appendix B.

A different student may show weaknesses in other areas. Pete, for example, may have many words under the section "Omissions." Perhaps he does not attempt to pronounce many of the words he does not recognize immediately. Pete may, therefore, need instruction in developing more effective strategies for anticipating words through the use of contextual and syntactic cues (see situations 2 and 3 in Appendix B).

Still another student may fail to recognize many word endings. Such miscues may be indicative of a possible problem in structural analysis (*s, es, ed, ing*, etc.). Teachers should remember, however, that some speakers of a particular dialect may omit word endings. Miscues of this type, as long as they make sense in the reader's dialect, should not be regarded as significant.

When analyzing word recognition by charting miscues, the teacher must be careful that any conclusions are based on patterns of miscues, not just a few miscues in any given category. It is generally recommended that only miscues at the student's independent and instructional levels be charted for analysis since the frustration level indicates that the reading process has broken down. The graded word lists can be used to estimate sight vocabulary and proficiency with phonics; however, a research study (Allington and McGill-Franzen, 1980) involving fourth graders revealed that students made different miscues when reading the same words in a random order instead of in context. Any conclusions or hypotheses the teacher makes in regard to a student's strengths and weaknesses in word attack should, therefore, be considered tentative and verified or discounted through classroom instruction. The teacher should also remember that word recognition is not an end in itself; it is a means for gaining an understanding of the material. It is often possible for a student to gain meaning from reading material even though he makes several miscues. Instruction in word recognition, therefore, should be based upon strategies that will help him understand a reading selection.

*Strategy 2: Advanced Qualitative Analysis.* A more advanced system for analyzing miscues has been developed by Christie (1979) and is presented in Table 15. This system draws upon the work of Goodman and Burke (1972) and the suggestions of Williamson and Young (1974). The following qualitative analysis has been adapted, with permission, from Christie. For convenience, the procedure is presented in a five-step outline form.

# Table 15
## System for the Qualitative Analysis of Miscues
### Analysis Sheet

| MISCUE | TEXT | GRAPHIC SIMILARITY | | | CONTEXT | | |
| | | Beginning | Middle | End | Acceptable | Unacceptable | Self-Correction |
|---|---|---|---|---|---|---|---|
| | | | | | | | |
| | | | | | | | |
| | | | | | | | |
| | | | | | | | |
| | | | | | | | |
| | | | | | | | |
| Column Total | | | | | | | |
| Number of Miscues Analyzed | | | | | | | |
| Percentage | | | | | | | |

### Profile Sheet

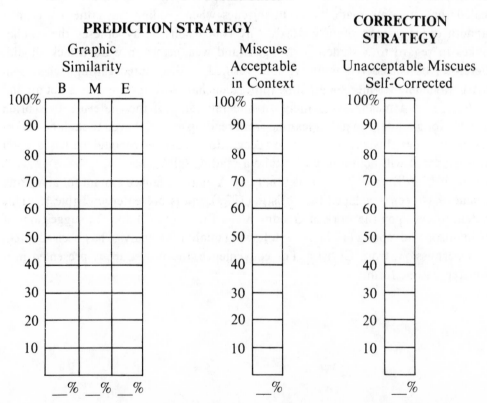

**PREDICTION STRATEGY**

Graphic Similarity

B  M  E

100%
90
80
70
60
50
40
30
20
10

__% __% __%

Miscues Acceptable in Context

100%
90
80
70
60
50
40
30
20
10

__%

**CORRECTION STRATEGY**

Unacceptable Miscues Self-Corrected

100%
90
80
70
60
50
40
30
20
10

__%

## Step 1—Select Miscues for Analysis

A. Select the following types of miscues for recording on the Analysis Sheet:
   1. substitutions
   2. omissions
   3. insertions
   4. word order reversals

B. Do *not* use the following types of miscues:
   1. repetitions
   2. hesitations
   3. prompts
   4. disregard for punctuation
   5. omissions of entire lines of text
   6. variations in pronunciation involving dialect

## Step 2—Record Miscues on the Analysis Sheet

A. Record each type of miscue as follows:
   1. substitutions

      The girl was very sad. (glad)

| MISCUE | TEXT |
|--------|------|
| glad | sad |

   2. omissions

      He went to (the) church.

| MISCUE | TEXT |
|--------|------|
| ——— | the |

   3. insertions

      The road was ^ narrow. (very)

| MISCUE | TEXT |
|--------|------|
| very | ——— |

   4. word order reversals

      Jill sat quietly at her desk. (at her desk quietly)

| MISCUE | TEXT |
|--------|------|
| at her desk quietly | quietly at her desk |

B. Special Rules
   1. Only record identical substitutions once.
   2. If the reader makes several attempts at a word, record the first complete word or non-word substitution.

      Example: He went up the stairs. (2. stars / 1. st-)

| MISCUE | TEXT |
|--------|------|
| stars | stairs |

   3. If a miscue causes the reader to immediately make another miscue, record as one complex miscue.

      Example: He could ^ dance all night. (have danced)

| | |
|--------|------|
| have danced | dance |

29

**Step 3—Analyze Miscues**

A. Graphic Similarity
  1. Miscues to analyze
    a. Only substitutions of a single word or non-word for a single text item should be analyzed for graphic similarity.
    b. Do *not* analyze omissions, insertions, reversals, or substitutions that involve more than one word. In these cases, draw *X's* through the three boxes under GRAPHIC SIMILARITY.
    c. Example:

    $\overset{\text{went}}{\text{He walked to (the) school.}}$

| MISCUE | TEXT | GRAPHIC SIMILARITY — Beginning | Middle | End |
|--------|------|:---:|:---:|:---:|
| went | walked | ✓ | | |
| ———— | the | ✕ | ✕ | ✕ |

  2. Judging graphic similarity
    a. Compare the sequence and shape of the letters in the miscue with those in the text item. Place a check in the appropriate box if the beginning, middle, and/or end of the miscue is graphically similar to the corresponding part of the text item.
    b. Guidelines
      (1) Divide the miscue and text item into corresponding thirds.
      (2) Use the following criteria for judging the different thirds as being graphically similar:
        (a) *Beginning* third—the first letter of the miscue and the first letter of the text item must be identical.
        (b) *Middle* and *End*—the letters in the miscue and text item need only be similar in sequence and configuration.
      (3) Special cases
        (a) Two-letter text items—place an *X* in the "Middle" box and judge only for beginning similarity.
        (b) One-letter text items—place an *X* in the "Middle" and "End" boxes and judge only for beginning similarity.

| MISCUE | TEXT | GRAPHIC SIMILARITY | | |
| --- | --- | --- | --- | --- |
| | | Beginning | Middle | End |
| men | man | ✓ | ✓ | ✓ |
| here | said | | | |
| his | this | | ✓ | ✓ |
| walk | walked | ✓ | ✓ | |
| cub | carry | ✓ | | |
| meal | material | ✓ | | ✓ |
| be | by | ✓ | ✕ | |
| if | it | ✓ | ✕ | ✓ |
| the | a | | ✕ | ✕ |

B. Acceptability in Context
  1. Judge all miscues recorded on the Analysis Sheet for acceptability in context.
  2. When judging the acceptability of a miscue, take the following two factors into consideration:
     a. *syntax*—Is the miscue grammatically acceptable in the context of the entire sentence?
     b. *semantics*—Does the miscue make sense in the context of the sentence and the preceding portion of the passage?
  3. Marking the Analysis Sheet
     a. If the miscue meets both criteria, check the box in the "Acceptable" column.
     b. If either criterion is not met, check the box in the "Unacceptable" column.

## C. Self-Correction

If the miscue is successfully self-corrected by the reader, place a check in the "Self-Correction" column.

| | Context | | Self-Correction |
|---|---|---|---|
| | Acceptable | Unacceptable | |
| Acceptable in context; self-correction | ✓ | | ✓ |
| Acceptable in context; no self-correction | ✓ | | |
| Unacceptable in context; self-correction | | ✓ | ✓ |
| Unacceptable in context; no self-correction | | ✓ | |

### Step 4—Determine Totals and Percentages

A. Graphic Similarity
   1. Count the number of checks in each column (Beginning, Middle, and End) and place the totals in the boxes marked COLUMN TOTAL.
   2. For each column, count the number of boxes that do not have X's in them. Place each total in the box marked NUMBER OF MISCUES ANALYZED.
   3. Determine the PERCENTAGE for each column by dividing each COLUMN TOTAL by the NUMBER OF MISCUES ANALYZED.
B. Acceptability in Context
   1. Count the number of checks in the "Acceptable" column and the number of checks in the "Unacceptable" column and enter each total in the appropriate COLUMN TOTAL box.
   2. "Acceptable" column *only*
      a. Enter the total number of miscues analyzed for acceptability in context in the box marked NUMBER OF MISCUES ANALYZED. (This should equal the total number of miscues recorded on the Analysis Sheet.)
      b. Determine the PERCENTAGE of miscues acceptable in context by dividing the COLUMN TOTAL by the NUMBER OF MISCUES ANALYZED.
C. Percentage of Unacceptable Miscues that Were Self-Corrected
   1. Count the number of miscues in the "Unacceptable" column that were self-corrected. (Be sure to count only self-corrections made on unacceptable miscues.) Place the total in the box marked COLUMN TOTAL.
   2. Determine the PERCENTAGE of unacceptable miscues that were self-corrected by dividing the COLUMN TOTAL by the total number of miscues that were unacceptable in context.

**Step 5—Complete Profile Sheet**

A. Transfer the percentages from the Analysis Sheet to the blanks below the appropriate bar graphs.

B. Darken in the bar graphs.

Once the three parts of the Profile Sheet have been completed, reading strategy lessons can be developed. The two Prediction Strategy graphs help to determine whether the student is relying on graphic cues, context cues, or both when predicting upcoming text and decoding unknown words. When both graphs are similar, the student has a balanced prediction strategy. If, on the other hand, the two graphs show a marked difference, the student may be depending excessively on one type of cue.

If the Graphic Similarity graph is high, and the Context graph is low, the student may be relying excessively on graphic (phonic) cues. If this is the case, reading strategy lessons that emphasize the use of context cues may be warranted. Several exercises suggested in situations 3 and 6 in Appendix B may be helpful.

When the Graphic Similarity graph is low and the Context graph is high, the student may be relying heavily on context cues. Strategy lessons could include asking the student a question like, "What word do you know that begins like _____ that would make sense?"

The Correction Strategy graph shows the percentage of unacceptable miscues that were self-corrected by the student. When a large percentage of unacceptable miscues are not corrected, strategy lessons to help the reader develop a sensitivity to correcting miscues that disrupt meaning may be needed. Situation 5 in Appendix B contains some useful suggestions. Several additional resources for reading strategy lessons can be found in the work of Allen and Watson (1976), Gillespie-Silver (1979), Maring (1978), and Spiegel (1978).

## Determining Strengths and Weaknesses in Comprehension

The Basic Reading Inventory contains five different types of comprehension questions coded as follows: (F) fact; (M) main idea; (E) evaluation; (I) inference; and (V) vocabulary. Two strategies are suggested for analyzing comprehension performance.

*Strategy 1: Analysis by Question Type.* The teacher can analyze errors in the various areas of comprehension after recording the number and types of questions the student misses on each passage read. An example of this procedure, using Dan's oral reading performance, is shown in Table 16. Using such a procedure may enable the teacher to discern patterns of difficulty in comprehension. Dan's errors on the comprehension questions marked in Table 16 indicate possible strengths in answering main idea and vocabulary questions. Areas of possible weakness include answering fact, evaluation, and inference questions. Because of the limited data upon which these hypotheses are based, Dan's silent reading should also be considered. These hypotheses should then be verified or discounted through instruction.

To determine Tony's possible strengths and weaknesses in comprehension, the teacher should complete Table 17 by determining the ratios of comprehension questions answered incorrectly and the corresponding percentages. First, record the

## Table 16
### Summary of Dan's Comprehension Performance in Oral Reading

| Grade | Fact (F-5)* Oral | Main Idea (M-1) Oral | Evaluation (E-1) Oral | Inference (I-2) Oral | Vocabulary (V-1) Oral |
|---|---|---|---|---|---|
| P | 1/5 | 0/1 | 0/1 | 0/2 | 0/1 |
| 1 | 1/5 | 0/1 | 0/1 | 0/2 | 0/1 |
| 2 | 2/5 | 0/1 | 0/1 | 1/2 | 0/1 |
| 3 | 2/5 | 0/1 | 1/1 | 1/2 | 1/1 |
| Ratio Incorrect | 6/20 | 0/4 | 1/4 | 2/8 | 0/4 |
| Percent Incorrect | 30% | 0% | 25% | 25% | 0% |

*Indicates the type of question and the number of questions in each graded paragraph. For example, F indicates a fact question and 5 signifies that each graded passage contains five F questions.

## Table 17
### Tony's Comprehension Performance in Oral Reading

| Grade | Fact (F-5) Oral | Main Idea (M-1) Oral | Evaluation (E-1) Oral | Inference (I-2) Oral | Vocabulary (V-1) Oral |
|---|---|---|---|---|---|
| 4 | 1/5 | 0/1 | 0/1 | 0/2 | 0/1 |
| 5 | 0/5 | 0/1 | 1/1 | 1/2 | 0/1 |
| 6 | 1/5 | 1/1 | 0/1 | 0/2 | 0/1 |
| 7 | 0/5 | 1/1 | 0/1 | 0/2 | 1/1 |
| 8 | 1/5 | 1/1 | 0/1 | 1/2 | 1/1 |
| Ratio Incorrect | 3/25 | /__ | /__ | /__ | /__ |
| Percent Incorrect | 12% | __% | __% | __% | __% |

number of questions answered and the number of errors the student made on that type of question. Second, determine the percent of errors by dividing the number of errors by the total number of that type of question and multiplying by 100. For example, Tony responded to 25 fact questions and missed 3 of them. His error rate for the fact questions was 12 percent (3 ÷ 25 = .12; .12 × 100 = 12%). What are Tony's possible strengths and weaknesses in comprehension?

Tony missed 3 of 25 fact questions (12%), 3 of 5 main idea questions (60%), 1 of 5 evaluation questions (20%), 2 of 10 inference questions (20%), and 2 of 5 vocabulary questions (40%). Based on these percentages, answering main idea and vocabulary questions may be hypothesized as areas of weakness. A possible strength is in the area of recalling facts. Evaluation and inference questions may also indicate areas of strength; however, it seems most appropriate from this analysis to identify errors in main idea and vocabulary questions as possible weaknesses and responses to fact questions as a possible strength.

When a student reads orally and silently, it is recommended that the results be combined for both sets of graded passages. This procedure enables the teacher to get a larger sample of behavior upon which to make judgments. Table 18 contains Tony's comprehension performance from the graded passages that were analyzed above, as well as his silent reading performance on a different set of graded passages from the Basic Reading Inventory. The teacher should complete Table 18 by determining the ratio of questions answered incorrectly and the corresponding per-

**Table 18**
Tony's Comprehension Performance in Oral and Silent Reading

| Grade | Fact (F-5) | | Main Idea (M-1) | | Evaluation (E-1) | | Inference (I-2) | | Vocabulary (V-1) | |
|---|---|---|---|---|---|---|---|---|---|---|
| | Oral | Silent | Oral | Silent | Oral | Silent | Oral | Silent | Oral | Silent |
| 4 | 1/5 | 0/5 | 0/1 | 0/1 | 0/1 | 0/1 | 0/2 | 1/2 | 0/1 | 0/1 |
| 5 | 0/5 | 0/5 | 0/1 | 0/1 | 1/1 | 0/1 | 1/2 | 0/2 | 0/1 | 0/1 |
| 6 | 1/5 | 1/5 | 1/1 | 1/1 | 0/1 | 0/1 | 0/2 | 1/2 | 0/1 | 1/1 |
| 7 | 0/5 | 3/5 | 1/1 | 0/1 | 0/1 | 0/1 | 0/2 | 0/2 | 1/1 | 0/1 |
| 8 | 1/5 | 2/5 | 1/1 | 1/1 | 0/1 | 0/1 | 1/2 | 0/2 | 1/1 | 1/1 |
| Ratio Incorrect | 3/25 | / | 3/5 | / | 1/5 | / | 2/10 | / | 2/5 | / |
| Percent Incorrect | 12 % | % | 60% | % | 20% | % | 20% | % | 40% | % |
| Average Percent Incorrect | | % | | % | | % | | % | | % |

| | Fact | | Main Idea | | Evaluation | | Inference | | Vocabulary | |
| --- | --- | --- | --- | --- | --- | --- | --- | --- | --- | --- |
| | Oral | Silent | Oral | Silent | Oral | Silent | Oral | Silent | Oral | Silent |
| Ratio Incorrect | 3/25 | 6/25 | 3/5 | 2/5 | 1/5 | 0/5 | 2/10 | 2/10 | 2/5 | 2/5 |
| Percent Incorrect | 12% | 24% | 60% | 40% | 20% | 0% | 20% | 20% | 40% | 40% |
| Average Percent Incorrect | 18% | | 50% | | 10% | | 20% | | 40% | |

centages. A comparison of Tony's oral and silent comprehension performance is shown in Table 19. The teacher should check her work and resolve any discrepancies. Since the number of questions upon which the total percentages are calculated has increased, the hypotheses about Tony's strengths and weaknesses should have greater validity. His answers to fact, evaluation, and inference questions appear to be areas of strength. Errors on main idea and vocabulary questions may be hypothesized as areas of weakness. Even though these findings are generally consistent with those based on Tony's oral reading, the combined analysis should give the teacher greater confidence in the results.

*Strategy 2: Analysis by Level of Comprehension.* A second way to analyze comprehension performance is by classifying the various types of comprehension questions into logical categories. Numerous classification schemes have been developed (Tatham, 1978). It is recommended that teachers use two levels of comprehension. Category one, lower-level comprehension, is comprised of the five fact questions. Category two, higher-level comprehension, is comprised of the main idea, evaluation, inference, and vocabulary questions. The logic behind the two categories is that the first is based on literal comprehension while the second is based on thinking beyond the ideas stated in the graded passages. The student's ability to reason and use experiences is assessed in the latter category. Other classification schemes are also possible; the teacher is encouraged to modify the scheme suggested to conform to her own conception of comprehension. The two categories of comprehension suggested make it possible for teachers to view comprehension globally when planning instruction for students. Table 20 contains the results of such an analysis for Tony's scores that were reported earlier.

The results of the global analysis reveal that Tony's major difficulties are in the higher-level comprehension area. If a more detailed analysis of this area is desired, the comprehension questions may be arranged by type (see p. 33) and the responses analyzed.

**Table 20**
Summary of Tony's Two-Level Comprehension Performance

| | Lower-Level Comprehension (Fact Questions Only) | | Higher-Level Comprehension (All Other Questions) | |
|---|---|---|---|---|
| | Oral | Silent | Oral | Silent |
| Ratio Incorrect | 3/25 | 6/25 | 8/25 | 6/25 |
| Total Ratio | 9/50 | | 14/50 | |
| Total Percent Incorrect | 18% | | 28% | |

## Summary

Users of this inventory should realize that the results from the Basic Reading Inventory are virtually useless unless they become blueprints for instruction. In fact, test results will not help a student improve his reading unless the teacher uses the insights from the tests in her teaching. It is of little value, for example, to determine that a student in the sixth grade has an instructional level of third grade if the teacher insists that he be given a sixth grade basal text to "read" since he is a sixth grader. Even if the teacher places this student in a third grade book, it is doubtful that maximum progress will be made in reading if his specific needs in reading are ignored. The *total* results from the Basic Reading Inventory must be used to help plan effective instruction, taking into account each student's *specific* difficulties in word recognition and/or comprehension.

Tests like the Basic Reading Inventory play a substantial role in providing data for placing students in appropriate instructional materials, diagnosing reading difficulties, and developing reading strategy lessons. Unless they are used in conjunction with observation, cumulative records, and other evaluative techniques, serious errors may result. One should not underestimate the importance of the Basic Reading Inventory for classroom and clinical use; however, the test results should be used to *guide* the teacher's responses to a student's reading. They should not be used to dictate a teacher's actions, thereby dominating her professional knowledge and experience. Professionals who use the Basic Reading Inventory as suggested in this manual will help insure that students are placed in appropriate reading materials and taught needed reading strategies.

# Bibliography

Allen, P. David and Dorothy J. Watson (eds.). *Findings of Research in Miscue Analysis: Classroom Implications.* Urbana, Illinois: National Council of Teachers of English, 1976.

Allington, Richard L. and Anne McGill-Franzen. "Word Identification Errors in Isolation and in Context: Apples vs. Oranges." *The Reading Teacher,* 33 (April, 1980), 795–800.

Betts, Emmett Albert. *Foundations of Reading Instruction.* New York: American Book Company, 1954.

Bond, Guy L. and Robert Dykstra. "The Cooperative Research Program in First-Grade Reading Instruction." *Reading Research Quarterly,* 2 (Summer, 1967), 5–142.

Christie, James F. "The Qualitative Analysis System: Updating the IRI." *Reading World,* 18 (May, 1979), 393–99.

Cohn, Marvin and Cynthia D'Alessandro. "When is a Decoding Error Not a Decoding Error?" *The Reading Teacher,* 32 (December, 1978), 341–44.

Dale, Edgar and Jeanne S. Chall. "A Formula for Predicting Readability: Instructions." *Educational Research Bulletin,* 27 (February 18, 1948), 37–54.

D'Angelo, Karen and Robert M. Wilson. "How Helpful is Insertion and Omission Miscue Analysis?" *The Reading Teacher,* 32 (February, 1979), 519–20.

Ekwall, Eldon E. "Informal Reading Inventories: The Instructional Level." *The Reading Teacher,* 29 (April, 1976), 662–65.

—————. "Should Repetitions Be Counted as Errors?" *The Reading Teacher,* 27 (January, 1974), 365–67.

Fry, Edward. "A Readability Formula That Saves Time." *Journal of Reading,* 11 (April, 1968), 513–16, 575–78.

Gillespie-Silver, Patricia. *Teaching Reading to Children with Special Needs.* Columbus, Ohio: Charles E. Merrill Publishing Company, 1979.

Goodman, Kenneth S. "A Linguistic Study of Cues and Miscues in Reading." *Elementary English,* 42 (October, 1965), 639–43.

—————. "The Search Called Reading." In Helen M. Robinson (ed.), *Coordinating Reading Instruction.* Glenview, Illinois: Scott, Foresman and Company, 1971, pp. 10–14.

Goodman, Yetta M. "Reading Diagnosis—Qualitative or Quantitative?" *The Reading Teacher,* 26 (October, 1972), 32–37.

Goodman, Yetta M. and Carolyn L. Burke. *Reading Miscue Inventory Manual: Procedure for Diagnosis and Evaluation.* New York: The Macmillan Company, 1972.

Hays, Warren S. "Criteria for the Instructional Level of Reading," 1975. Microfiche ED 117 665.

Hood, Joyce. "Is Miscue Analysis Practical for Teachers?" *The Reading Teacher,* 32 (December, 1978), 260–66.

Jacobs, H. Donald and Lyndon W. Searfoss. *Diagnostic Reading Inventory* (2nd ed.). Dubuque, Iowa: Kendall/Hunt Publishing Company, 1979.

Johns, Jerry L. "Informal Reading Inventories: A Survey Among Professionals." *Illinois School Research and Development,* 13 (Fall, 1976), 35–39.

Johnson, Marjorie Seddon and Roy A. Kress. *Informal Reading Inventories.* Newark, Delaware: International Reading Association, 1965.

Lipton, Aaron. "Miscalling While Reading Aloud: A Point of View." *The Reading Teacher,* 25 (May, 1972), 759–62.

Maring, Gerald H. "Matching Remediation to Miscues." *The Reading Teacher,* 31 (May, 1978), 887–91.

Marzano, Robert J., Jean Larson, Geri Tish, and Sue Vodehnal. "The Graded Word List is Not a Shortcut to an IRI." *The Reading Teacher,* 31 (March, 1978), 647–51.

Newman, Harold. "Oral Reading Miscue Analysis is Good But Not Complete." *The Reading Teacher,* 31 (May, 1978), 883–86.

Pflaum, Susanna W. "Diagnosis of Oral Reading." *The Reading Teacher,* 33 (December, 1979), 278–84.

Pikulski, John. "A Critical Review: Informal Reading Inventories." *The Reading Teacher,* 28 (November, 1974), 141–51.

Powell, William R. "The Validity of the Instructional Reading Level." In Robert E. Leibert (ed.), *Diagnostic Viewpoints in Reading.* Newark, Delaware: International Reading Association, 1971, pp. 121–33.

Recht, Donna R. "The Self-Correction Process in Reading." *The Reading Teacher,* 29 (April, 1976), 632–36.

Rutherford, William L. "Five Steps to Effective Reading Instruction." *The Reading Teacher,* 24 (February, 1971), 416–21, 424.

Schlieper, Anne. "Oral Reading Errors in Relation to Grade and Level of Skill." *The Reading Teacher,* 31 (December, 1977), 283–87.

Spache, George D. *Diagnosing and Correcting Reading Disabilities.* Boston: Allyn and Bacon, Inc., 1976.

———. *Good Reading for Poor Readers.* Champaign, Illinois: Garrard Publishing Company, 1974.

Spiegel, Dixie Lee. "Meaning-Seeking Strategies for the Beginning Reader." *The Reading Teacher,* 31 (April, 1978), 772–76.

Tatham, Susan Masland. "Comprehension Taxonomies: Their Uses and Abuses." *The Reading Teacher,* 32 (November, 1978), 190–94.

Taylor, Stanford, Helen Frackenpohl, and James L. Pettee. *Grade Level Norms for the Components of the Fundamental Reading Skill* (Research Bulletin 3). New York: Educational Developmental Laboratories, a Division of McGraw-Hill Book Company, 1960.

Williamson, Leon E. and Freda Young. "The IRI and RMI Diagnostic Concepts Should be Synthesized." *Journal of Reading Behavior,* 5 (July, 1974), 183–94.

# BASIC
# READING
# INVENTORY

# Basic Reading Inventory, Form A

Graded Word Lists
Graded Passages

| List A-A | List A | List A 1417 | List A 8224 |
|----------|--------|-------------|-------------|
| 1. and | 1. ask | 1. faster | 1. family |
| 2. blue | 2. bad | 2. sleep | 2. quietly |
| 3. let | 3. face | 3. time | 3. smell |
| 4. tree | 4. something | 4. grow | 4. wishing |
| 5. go | 5. went | 5. again | 5. bottom |
| 6. my | 6. laughed | 6. your | 6. everyone |
| 7. at | 7. birthday | 7. much | 7. lamb |
| 8. look | 8. new | 8. told | 8. year |
| 9. up | 9. his | 9. please | 9. high |
| 10. red | 10. reads | 10. came | 10. started |
| 11. for | 11. wagon | 11. never | 11. teacher |
| 12. the | 12. but | 12. after | 12. always |
| 13. if | 13. soon | 13. then | 13. enough |
| 14. where | 14. they | 14. wonderful | 14. castle |
| 15. bed | 15. eat | 15. buzzard | 15. that's |
| 16. very | 16. matter | 16. trucks | 16. afraid |
| 17. here | 17. train | 17. before | 17. shout |
| 18. that | 18. into | 18. thought | 18. drink |
| 19. is | 19. white | 19. over | 19. gone |
| 20. what | 20. children | 20. sled | 20. country |

## List A 3183

1. company
2. escape
3. conductor
4. scampered
5. anxious
6. chewed
7. electric
8. hundred
9. discover
10. weather
11. chickens
12. favorite
13. because
14. able
15. reason
16. borrow
17. mind
18. danger
19. crawl
20. distance

## List A 5414

1. falsehood
2. level
3. capture
4. metal
5. vanishing
6. serious
7. observing
8. automobile
9. swoop
10. target
11. ought
12. double
13. balanced
14. predict
15. platform
16. language
17. force
18. impossible
19. island
20. harbor

## List A 5895

1. expert
2. instant
3. wisdom
4. omitted
5. enormous
6. heighten
7. approved
8. dense
9. voyage
10. future
11. document
12. terrific
13. patience
14. dusk
15. satisfied
16. shrill
17. remarkably
18. bullets
19. catalog
20. generosity

## List A 6687

1. ankle
2. establishment
3. violent
4. fragments
5. legend
6. amount
7. confidence
8. glittering
9. interior
10. application
11. teamwork
12. shifted
13. barter
14. devote
15. sausages
16. transportation
17. assemble
18. arrangement
19. emergency
20. calmly

## List A 7371

1. caboose
2. timbers
3. excerpt
4. dialect
5. penalty
6. unexplored
7. alternately
8. geologist
9. render
10. biscuit
11. conservative
12. symptoms
13. carbonate
14. wavelengths
15. complexion
16. broth
17. perpetual
18. condenses
19. proportional
20. enrollment

## List A 1883

1. attendants
2. breakthrough
3. whimpered
4. legible
5. discolored
6. reconstruction
7. admiral
8. circulatory
9. saxophone
10. turbulent
11. nightingale
12. clarify
13. baboon
14. crag
15. potent
16. controversial
17. metaphor
18. integration
19. anticipated
20. gouge

It was fall. Ann went for a walk. She took her dog Sam. They liked to walk. They walked for a long time. They saw trees. Some were red. Some were green. They were pretty. Ann and Sam saw birds too. Sam did not run after them. He was nice.

Jack woke up Saturday morning. He looked out of the window. The ground was white. The trees were white.

"Oh boy," said Jack, "snow."

"What did you say?" asked Tom, rubbing his eyes.

"It snowed last night. Get up and see," said Jack.

Both boys ran to the window.

"Look at that!" said Tom. "Come on. Let's get dressed."

Jack and Tom ran into the kitchen.

"Mom!" they said. "It snowed last night."

"Yes," said Mom. "Dad went out to get your sleds. First we will eat breakfast. Then we can have some fun. The first snow is the best!"

A

One day Spotty went for a walk. The sun was warm. Spotty walked to the pond. There he saw a frog. The frog was on a log. Spotty wanted to play. Spotty began to bark. The frog just sat.

Spotty jumped into the water. The frog jumped in too. Then Spotty did not know what to do. The water was very deep. It went way over his head. Spotty moved his legs. Soon his head came out of the water. He kept on moving. He came to the other side of the pond. That is how Spotty learned to swim.

A 1417

It was the first time Bill went to camp. He was very happy to be there. Soon he went for a walk in the woods to look for many kinds of leaves. He found leaves from some maple and oak trees. As Bill walked in the woods, he saw some animal tracks. At that moment, a mouse ran into a small hole by a tree. Bill wondered if the tracks were made by the mouse. He looked around for other animals. He did not see any. The only thing Bill saw was an old bird's nest in a pine tree.

A 8224

The bees had been making honey all day long. At night it was cool and calm. I had slept well until I heard a loud noise near my window. It sounded as if someone were trying to break into my cabin. As I moved from my cot, I could see something black standing near the window. In fright I knocked on the window. Very slowly and quietly the great shadow moved down and went away. The next day we found bear tracks. The bear had come for the honey that the bees were making in the attic of the cabin.

A 3183

Many years ago, people made up stories about things in nature they could not explain. These ancient stories are called myths. Some stories were about lightning. Some were about thunder. Others were about the seas and the oceans. Sometimes people saw pictures in the clouds and among the stars. They made up stories about these pictures and told them to their children. When their children grew up, they told the stories to their children. That is why we still hear myths. But today we know more of the reasons why things happen in our world, so there are fewer myths.

A 5414

49

My uncle and I went camping last week. We left home Friday after school and reached our campsite Friday night. After setting up our tent we went to bed. I could not fall asleep because I was eager to go trout fishing for the first time in my life. Finally I fell asleep only to be shaken by my uncle informing me it was time for breakfast. I got up out of my sleeping bag, got dressed, and trudged out to the blazing fire. I devoured a breakfast of bacon and eggs that Uncle Joe had prepared on the fire.

A 5895

The heavy fog swept across a pumpkin field where the Great Orange Witch lived in her shady hut. At night dim lights were seen in the cloudy windows and odd sounds drifted out from under doors and through cracks in the walls. No one had ever seen the witch, but kids imagined her to look like any other sorceress. They were sadly mistaken. She was no ordinary witch but one who decided the fate of weather on Halloween Eve. If the witch thought that it should storm on Halloween, she would drop more grape jelly beans in her evil brew.

One of the most beloved tales is of the princess and her knight. The princess, shackled to a rock, caught the eye of the wandering knight. He galloped over and, with a single stroke of his sword, released her from the iron chain. Taking her hand, he led her away from the dreadful confinement of the rock. While relaxing in a sunny meadow, he comforted her with reassuring words. The princess told him that she had been seized by pirates. Later, she had been brought to this savage island as a peace offering to the terrible monsters of the sea.

The mountain loomed ominously in the foreground. There it was, the lonely unconquered giant, Mt. Kilarma. In sheer size there was nothing imposing about the 15,000 foot height of Mt. Kilarma. The dangers rested in the skirt of glaciers around the steep sides of the mountain and the fiercely changing winds that tore at the summit. Many had tried to defeat this magnificent creation of nature, but to date no one had. Mindful of this, the band of mountaineers stared at the huge mass of ice. Could they reach the mountain's peak and do what no one had ever accomplished?

# Basic Reading Inventory: Performance Booklet
## (Form A)

*Jerry L. Johns*
*Northern Illinois University*

Student _____   Sex   M   F   Date of Testing _____

School _____ Grade _____   Date of Birth _____

Teacher _____   Examiner _____

| | SUMMARY OF STUDENT'S PERFORMANCE | | | | | |
|---|---|---|---|---|---|---|
| | Word Recognition | | Comprehension | | | Listening |
| Grade | Isolation | Context | Oral Reading Form A B C | Silent Reading Form A B C | | Form A B C |
| | Total Score / Level | Percent Correct / Level | Percent Correct / Level | Percent Correct / Level / Rate | | Percent Correct / Level |
| PP | | | | | | |
| P | | | | | | |
| 1 | | | | | | |
| 2 | | | | | | |
| 3 | | | | | | |
| 4 | | | | | | |
| 5 | | | | | | |
| 6 | | | | | | |
| 7 | | | | | | |
| 8 | | | | | | |

**Estimated Levels**

Independent _____

Instructional _____

Frustration _____

Listening _____

**General Criteria for Reading Levels**

| | *Ind.* | *Inst.* | *Frust.* |
|---|---|---|---|
| Word Recognition (Isolation) | 19–20 | 14–18 | ≤ 13 |
| Word Recognition (Context) | 99 | 95 | 90 |
| Comprehension | 90 | 75 | 50 |

**KENDALL/HUNT PUBLISHING COMPANY**
Dubuque, Iowa

## SUMMARY OF ADMINISTRATION
## AND SCORING PROCEDURES

To determine a student's independent, instructional, and frustration levels, administer the three reading tests included in the Basic Reading Inventory as follows:

**WORD RECOGNITION IN ISOLATION:** Select a graded word list at a reading level that will be easy for the student. Ask the student to pronounce the words rapidly. Record the student's responses in the timed column beside the corresponding word list in the performance booklet.

Return to mispronounced or unknown words for a second attempt at analysis, and note the student's responses in the untimed column. Administer successive word lists until the student is no longer able to achieve a total score of at least fourteen correct words or until the student becomes frustrated.

**Scoring:** Total the correct responses in the timed and untimed columns. Consult the criteria on the general scoring guide shown below to determine the reading level achieved on each graded word list. Record the number-correct scores and the reading levels on the summary sheet of the performance booklet.

**WORD RECOGNITION IN CONTEXT:** Ask the student to read aloud the passage graded one level *below* the highest independent level achieved on the graded word lists. As the student reads the passage, record all miscues such as omissions, repetitions, substitutions, etc. on the corresponding copy of the passage found in the performance booklet.

**Scoring:** To find the percent-correct score, count the number of significant miscues (those that affect meaning) in each graded passage. At the pre-primer level, each significant miscue is valued at 2 percentage points and subtracted from 100. At the primer level and above, each significant miscue is valued at 1 percentage point and subtracted from 100.

To determine reading levels from the percent-correct scores, consult the criteria on the general scoring guide shown below. Record the percent-correct scores and the reading levels on the summary sheet of the performance booklet.

**COMPREHENSION:** Ask the comprehension questions that are beside the passage in the performance booklet and record the student's responses. Continue administering graded passages until the student has ten or more significant word recognition miscues, is unable to answer half the comprehension questions, or demonstrates behavior associated with frustration.

**Scoring:** To find the percent-correct score achieved on each passage, divide the number of correct responses by the number of questions.

To convert the percent-correct scores into reading levels, consult the criteria on the general scoring guide below. (Teacher judgment must be exercised at the pre-primer level because the limited number of questions may not permit precise measurement of achievement.) Record the percent-correct scores and the reading levels on the summary sheet of the performance booklet.

### General Scoring Guide for Reading Levels

| Subtest of Basic Reading Inventory | Independent Level | Independent or Instructional Level | Instructional Level | Instructional or Frustration Level | Frustration Level |
|---|---|---|---|---|---|
| Word Recognition in Isolation | 20–19 | | 18–14 | | 13 or less |
| Word Recognition in Context (%) | 99 | 98–96 | 95 | 94–91 | 90 or less |
| Comprehension (%) | 90 | 85–80 | 75 | 70–55 | 50 or less |

Note: Teacher judgment is necessary in gray areas.

| List A-A | Timed | Untimed | List A | Timed | Untimed |
|----------|-------|---------|--------|-------|---------|
| 1. and | \_\_\_\_ | \_\_\_\_ | 1. ask | \_\_\_\_ | \_\_\_\_ |
| 2. blue | \_\_\_\_ | \_\_\_\_ | 2. bad | \_\_\_\_ | \_\_\_\_ |
| 3. let | \_\_\_\_ | \_\_\_\_ | 3. face | \_\_\_\_ | \_\_\_\_ |
| 4. tree | \_\_\_\_ | \_\_\_\_ | 4. something | \_\_\_\_ | \_\_\_\_ |
| 5. go | \_\_\_\_ | \_\_\_\_ | 5. went | \_\_\_\_ | \_\_\_\_ |
| 6. my | \_\_\_\_ | \_\_\_\_ | 6. laughed | \_\_\_\_ | \_\_\_\_ |
| 7. at | \_\_\_\_ | \_\_\_\_ | 7. birthday | \_\_\_\_ | \_\_\_\_ |
| 8. look | \_\_\_\_ | \_\_\_\_ | 8. new | \_\_\_\_ | \_\_\_\_ |
| 9. up | \_\_\_\_ | \_\_\_\_ | 9. his | \_\_\_\_ | \_\_\_\_ |
| 10. red | \_\_\_\_ | \_\_\_\_ | 10. reads | \_\_\_\_ | \_\_\_\_ |
| 11. for | \_\_\_\_ | \_\_\_\_ | 11. wagon | \_\_\_\_ | \_\_\_\_ |
| 12. the | \_\_\_\_ | \_\_\_\_ | 12. but | \_\_\_\_ | \_\_\_\_ |
| 13. if | \_\_\_\_ | \_\_\_\_ | 13. soon | \_\_\_\_ | \_\_\_\_ |
| 14. where | \_\_\_\_ | \_\_\_\_ | 14. they | \_\_\_\_ | \_\_\_\_ |
| 15. bed | \_\_\_\_ | \_\_\_\_ | 15. eat | \_\_\_\_ | \_\_\_\_ |
| 16. very | \_\_\_\_ | \_\_\_\_ | 16. matter | \_\_\_\_ | \_\_\_\_ |
| 17. here | \_\_\_\_ | \_\_\_\_ | 17. train | \_\_\_\_ | \_\_\_\_ |
| 18. that | \_\_\_\_ | \_\_\_\_ | 18. into | \_\_\_\_ | \_\_\_\_ |
| 19. is | \_\_\_\_ | \_\_\_\_ | 19. white | \_\_\_\_ | \_\_\_\_ |
| 20. what | \_\_\_\_ | \_\_\_\_ | 20. children | \_\_\_\_ | \_\_\_\_ |

Number Correct _____ _____ Number Correct _____ _____

Total Score _____ Total Score _____

### Scoring Guide for Graded Word Lists

| Independent | Instructional | Frustration |
|-------------|---------------|-------------|
| 20 19 | 18 17 16 15 14 | 13 or less |

| List A 1417 | Timed | Untimed | List A 8224 | Timed | Untimed |
|---|---|---|---|---|---|
| 1. faster | _____ | _____ | 1. family | _____ | _____ |
| 2. sleep | _____ | _____ | 2. quietly | _____ | _____ |
| 3. time | _____ | _____ | 3. smell | _____ | _____ |
| 4. grow | _____ | _____ | 4. wishing | _____ | _____ |
| 5. again | _____ | _____ | 5. bottom | _____ | _____ |
| 6. your | _____ | _____ | 6. everyone | _____ | _____ |
| 7. much | _____ | _____ | 7. lamb | _____ | _____ |
| 8. told | _____ | _____ | 8. year | _____ | _____ |
| 9. please | _____ | _____ | 9. high | _____ | _____ |
| 10. came | _____ | _____ | 10. started | _____ | _____ |
| 11. never | _____ | _____ | 11. teacher | _____ | _____ |
| 12. after | _____ | _____ | 12. always | _____ | _____ |
| 13. then | _____ | _____ | 13. enough | _____ | _____ |
| 14. wonderful | _____ | _____ | 14. castle | _____ | _____ |
| 15. buzzard | _____ | _____ | 15. that's | _____ | _____ |
| 16. trucks | _____ | _____ | 16. afraid | _____ | _____ |
| 17. before | _____ | _____ | 17. shout | _____ | _____ |
| 18. thought | _____ | _____ | 18. drink | _____ | _____ |
| 19. over | _____ | _____ | 19. gone | _____ | _____ |
| 20. sled | _____ | _____ | 20. country | _____ | _____ |
| Number Correct | _____ | _____ | Number Correct | _____ | _____ |
| Total Score | _____ | | Total Score | _____ | |

### Scoring Guide for Graded Word Lists

| Independent | Instructional | Frustration |
|---|---|---|
| 20 19 | 18 17 16 15 14 | 13 or less |

| List A 3183 | Timed | Untimed | List A 5414 | Timed | Untimed |
|---|---|---|---|---|---|
| 1. company | _____ | _____ | 1. falsehood | _____ | _____ |
| 2. escape | _____ | _____ | 2. level | _____ | _____ |
| 3. conductor | _____ | _____ | 3. capture | _____ | _____ |
| 4. scampered | _____ | _____ | 4. metal | _____ | _____ |
| 5. anxious | _____ | _____ | 5. vanishing | _____ | _____ |
| 6. chewed | _____ | _____ | 6. serious | _____ | _____ |
| 7. electric | _____ | _____ | 7. observing | _____ | _____ |
| 8. hundred | _____ | _____ | 8. automobile | _____ | _____ |
| 9. discover | _____ | _____ | 9. swoop | _____ | _____ |
| 10. weather | _____ | _____ | 10. target | _____ | _____ |
| 11. chickens | _____ | _____ | 11. ought | _____ | _____ |
| 12. favorite | _____ | _____ | 12. double | _____ | _____ |
| 13. because | _____ | _____ | 13. balanced | _____ | _____ |
| 14. able | _____ | _____ | 14. predict | _____ | _____ |
| 15. reason | _____ | _____ | 15. platform | _____ | _____ |
| 16. borrow | _____ | _____ | 16. language | _____ | _____ |
| 17. mind | _____ | _____ | 17. force | _____ | _____ |
| 18. danger | _____ | _____ | 18. impossible | _____ | _____ |
| 19. crawl | _____ | _____ | 19. island | _____ | _____ |
| 20. distance | _____ | _____ | 20. harbor | _____ | _____ |
| Number Correct | _____ | _____ | Number Correct | _____ | _____ |
| Total Score | | _____ | Total Score | | _____ |

## Scoring Guide for Graded Word Lists

| Independent | Instructional | Frustration |
|---|---|---|
| 20 19 | 18 17 16 15 14 | 13 or less |

| List A 5895 | Timed | Untimed | List A 6687 | Timed | Untimed |
|---|---|---|---|---|---|
| 1. expert | | | 1. ankle | | |
| 2. instant | | | 2. establishment | | |
| 3. wisdom | | | 3. violent | | |
| 4. omitted | | | 4. fragments | | |
| 5. enormous | | | 5. legend | | |
| 6. heighten | | | 6. amount | | |
| 7. approved | | | 7. confidence | | |
| 8. dense | | | 8. glittering | | |
| 9. voyage | | | 9. interior | | |
| 10. future | | | 10. application | | |
| 11. document | | | 11. teamwork | | |
| 12. terrific | | | 12. shifted | | |
| 13. patience | | | 13. barter | | |
| 14. dusk | | | 14. devote | | |
| 15. satisfied | | | 15. sausages | | |
| 16. shrill | | | 16. transportation | | |
| 17. remarkably | | | 17. assemble | | |
| 18. bullets | | | 18. arrangement | | |
| 19. catalog | | | 19. emergency | | |
| 20. generosity | | | 20. calmly | | |
| Number Correct | | | Number Correct | | |
| Total Score | | | Total Score | | |

### Scoring Guide for Graded Word Lists

| Independent | Instructional | Frustration |
|---|---|---|
| 20 19 | 18 17 16 15 14 | 13 or less |

| List A 7371 | Timed | Untimed | List A 1883 | Timed | Untimed |
|---|---|---|---|---|---|
| 1. caboose | _____ | _____ | 1. attendants | _____ | _____ |
| 2. timbers | _____ | _____ | 2. breakthrough | _____ | _____ |
| 3. excerpt | _____ | _____ | 3. whimpered | _____ | _____ |
| 4. dialect | _____ | _____ | 4. legible | _____ | _____ |
| 5. penalty | _____ | _____ | 5. discolored | _____ | _____ |
| 6. unexplored | _____ | _____ | 6. reconstruction | _____ | _____ |
| 7. alternately | _____ | _____ | 7. admiral | _____ | _____ |
| 8. geologist | _____ | _____ | 8. circulatory | _____ | _____ |
| 9. render | _____ | _____ | 9. saxophone | _____ | _____ |
| 10. biscuit | _____ | _____ | 10. turbulent | _____ | _____ |
| 11. conservative | _____ | _____ | 11. nightingale | _____ | _____ |
| 12. symptoms | _____ | _____ | 12. clarify | _____ | _____ |
| 13. carbonate | _____ | _____ | 13. baboon | _____ | _____ |
| 14. wavelengths | _____ | _____ | 14. crag | _____ | _____ |
| 15. complexion | _____ | _____ | 15. potent | _____ | _____ |
| 16. broth | _____ | _____ | 16. controversial | _____ | _____ |
| 17. perpetual | _____ | _____ | 17. metaphor | _____ | _____ |
| 18. condenses | _____ | _____ | 18. integration | _____ | _____ |
| 19. proportional | _____ | _____ | 19. anticipated | _____ | _____ |
| 20. enrollment | _____ | _____ | 20. gouge | _____ | _____ |

Number Correct _____ _____          Number Correct _____ _____

Total Score _____          Total Score _____

### Scoring Guide for Graded Word Lists

| Independent | Instructional | Frustration |
|---|---|---|
| 20 19 | 18 17 16 15 14 | 13 or less |

F 1. ___ What time of the year or season was it?
(fall)

F 2. ___ What did Ann do?
(took her dog for a walk)

E 3. ___ Why do you think Ann took her dog on the walk?
(any logical response; for company)

I 4. ___ Why do you think Sam didn't run after the birds?
(any logical response; he knew they would fly away)

V 5. ___ What does "nice" mean?
(pleasant; enjoyable; pleasing, etc.)

Percent of Comprehension ____

It was fall. Ann went for a walk. She took her dog Sam. They liked to walk. They walked for a long time. They saw trees. Some were red. Some were green. They were pretty. Ann and Sam saw birds too. Sam did not run after them. He was nice.

Percent of Word Recognition ____

$3000 \overline{\smash{\big)}\phantom{0000}}$ WPM

## Scoring Guide: Pre-Primer

Percent of Word Recognition in Context

| 100 99 | 98 97 96 | 95 | 94 93 92 91 | 90 or less |
|---|---|---|---|---|
| Independent Level | Independent or Instructional | Instructional Level | Instructional or Frustration | Frustration Level |
| 100 95 90 | 85 80 | 75 | 70 65 60 55 | 50 or less |

Percent of Comprehension

A

M 1. ___ What is this story about?
(boys getting ready to play in the snow)

F 2. ___ On what day does the story take place?
(Saturday)

F 3. ___ What happened when the boys woke up?
(they ran to the window; they saw snow)

F 4. ___ How did the trees look?
(white)

F 5. ___ What was Dad doing?
(getting the sleds)

F 6. ___ Why didn't they go outside right away?
(they had to get dressed and eat breakfast)

I 7. ___ Why do you think the boys were so excited?
(any logical response; they will play in the snow)

I 8. ___ What do you think Mom meant when she said that the first snow is the best?
(any logical response)

E 9. ___ What things do you think the family will do outside?
(any logical response; make snowballs; go sledding, etc.)

V 10. ___ What is "ground"?
(something you walk on)

Percent of Comprehension ____

Jack woke up Saturday morning. He looked out of the window. The ground was white. The trees were white.

"Oh boy," said Jack, "snow."

"What did you say?" asked Tom, rubbing his eyes.

"It snowed last night. Get up and see," said Jack.

Both boys ran to the window.

"Look at that!" said Tom. "Come on. Let's get dressed."

Jack and Tom ran into the kitchen.

"Mom!" they said. "It snowed last night."

"Yes," said Mom. "Dad went out to get your sleds. First we will eat breakfast. Then we can have some fun. The first snow is the best!"

Percent of Word Recognition ____

____ WPM
)6000

## Scoring Guide: Primer

Percent of Word Recognition in Context

| 100 99 | 98 97 96 | 95 | 94 93 92 91 | 90 or less |
|---|---|---|---|---|
| Independent Level | Independent or Instructional | Instructional Level | Instructional or Frustration | Frustration Level |
| 100 95 90 | 85 80 | 75 | 70 65 60 55 | 50 or less |

Percent of Comprehension

63

M  1. ___  What is this story about?
(Spotty and a frog; how Spotty learned to swim)

F  2. ___  Where did Spotty go?
(to the pond; for a walk)

F  3. ___  What did Spotty see?
(a frog)

F  4. ___  What happened when Spotty saw the frog?
(he barked; he wanted to play; the frog just sat [any one])

F  5. ___  What did Spotty do when the water went over his head?
(moved his legs; he didn't know what to do)

F  6. ___  What did Spotty learn in this story?
(how to swim)

I  7. ___  Why do you think the frog jumped into the water?
(any logical response; to get away from Spotty)

I  8. ___  Who was Spotty?
(any logical response; a dog)

E  9. ___  Why do you think Spotty wanted to play with the frog?
(any logical response; he was lonesome)

V  10. ___  What is a "pond"?
(like a lake, etc.)

Percent of Comprehension ____

One day Spotty went for a walk. The sun was warm. Spotty walked to the pond. There he saw a frog. The frog was on a log. Spotty wanted to play. Spotty began to bark. The frog just sat.

Spotty jumped into the water. The frog jumped in too. Then Spotty did not know what to do. The water was very deep. It went way over his head. Spotty moved his legs. Soon his head came out of the water. He kept on moving. He came to the other side of the pond. That is how Spotty learned to swim.

Percent of Word Recognition ____

$\overline{)6000}$ ____ WPM

### Scoring Guide: One

Percent of Word Recognition in Context

| 100 99 | 98 97 96 | 95 | 94 93 92 91 | 90 or less |
|---|---|---|---|---|
| Independent Level | Independent or Instructional | Instructional Level | Instructional or Frustration | Frustration Level |
| 100 95 90 | 85 80 | 75 | 70 65 60 55 | 50 or less |

Percent of Comprehension

M   1. ___   What is this story about?
            (a boy at camp; Bill's walk in the
            woods)

F   2. ___   Why did Bill go walking in the woods?
            (to look for leaves)

F   3. ___   Did Bill enjoy going to camp? How do
            you know?
            (yes, the story said he was happy there)

F   4. ___   What kinds of leaves did Bill find in
            the woods?
            (maple and oak leaves)

F   5. ___   Where did the mouse go?
            (into a small hole by a tree)

F   6. ___   What else did Bill see besides the
            mouse?
            (a bird's nest and animal tracks)

I   7. ___   Do you think Bill went on this walk by
            himself? What makes you think so?
            (any logical response)

I   8. ___   Why do you think Bill was happy at
            camp?
            (any logical response)

E   9. ___   Do you think it is important for boys
            and girls to go to camp? Why?
            (any logical response)

V   10. ___  What are "tracks"?
            (footprints made in the dirt; something
            made by animals when they walk or
            run)

Percent of Comprehension ____

It was the first time Bill went to camp. He was very happy to be there. Soon he went for a walk in the woods to look for many kinds of leaves. He found leaves from some maple and oak trees. As Bill walked in the woods, he saw some animal tracks. At that moment, a mouse ran into a small hole by a tree. Bill wondered if the tracks were made by the mouse. He looked around for other animals. He did not see any. The only thing Bill saw was an old bird's nest in a pine tree.

Percent of Word Recognition ____

$6000 \div$ ____ WPM

## Scoring Guide: Two

### Percent of Word Recognition in Context

| 100 99 | 98 97 96 | 95 | 94 93 92 91 | 90 or less |
|---|---|---|---|---|
| Independent Level | Independent or Instructional | Instructional Level | Instructional or Frustration | Frustration Level |
| 100 95 90 | 85 80 | 75 | 70 65 60 55 | 50 or less |

Percent of Comprehension

M 1. ___ What is this story about?
(a bear trying to get honey; being scared)

F 2. ___ What were the bees doing?
(making honey)

F 3. ___ What happened to the person in this story?
(the person was awakened by a loud noise at the window)

F 4. ___ What was standing near the window?
(blackness; a shadow; a bear)

F 5. ___ What was found the next day?
(bear tracks)

F 6. ___ Where were the bees making honey?
(in the attic of the cabin)

I 7. ___ How did the person probably feel the next day? Why?
(any logical response; relieved; frightened)

I 8. ___ Why do you think the bear walked away?
(any logical response; it heard the knock)

E 9. ___ What would you do if you heard scratching on your window?
(any logical response; call someone)

V 10. ___ What is an "attic"?
(a place way upstairs in your house where you put junk and stuff)

Percent of Comprehension ___

The bees had been making honey all day long. At night it was cool and calm. I had slept well until I heard a loud noise near my window. It sounded as if someone were trying to break into my cabin. As I moved from my cot, I could see something black standing near the window. In fright I knocked on the window. Very slowly and quietly the great shadow moved down and went away. The next day we found bear tracks. The bear had come for the honey that the bees were making in the attic of the cabin.

Percent of Word Recognition ___

___ WPM
$\overline{)6000}$

## Scoring Guide: Three

Percent of Word Recognition in Context

| 100 99 | 98 97 96 | 95 | 94 93 92 91 | 90 or less |
|---|---|---|---|---|
| Independent Level | Independent or Instructional | Instructional Level | Instructional or Frustration | Frustration Level |
| 100 95 90 | 85 80 | 75 | 70 65 60 55 | 50 or less |

Percent of Comprehension

M 1. ___ What is this story about?
(myths; people told stories about things they couldn't explain)

F 2. ___ What are ancient stories called?
(myths)

F 3. ___ What were the stories often about?
(lightning; thunder; oceans; seas; clouds; [any two])

F 4. ___ Why did people make up myths?
(to explain things they didn't understand)

F 5. ___ Why do we still hear myths?
(because they are passed down to the children)

F 6. ___ What was special about some stars?
(they made pictures people told stories about)

I 7. ___ How long ago do you think myths were made up? Why?
(any logical response; as early as cave men)

I 8. ___ What qualities would a person need to tell myths?
(any logical response; good memory; interesting)

E 9. ___ Do you think the children believed the stories told about what happened in nature? Why?
(any logical response)

V 10. ___ What is "nature"?
(the things that make up our world)

Percent of Comprehension ___

Many years ago, people made up stories about things in nature they could not explain. These ancient stories are called myths. Some stories were about lightning. Some were about thunder. Others were about the seas and the oceans. Sometimes people saw pictures in the clouds and among the stars. They made up stories about these pictures and told them to their children. When their children grew up, they told the stories to their children. That is why we still hear myths. But today we know more of the reasons why things happen in our world, so there are fewer myths.

Percent of Word Recognition ___

____ WPM
6000 ⟌

### Scoring Guide: Four

Percent of Word Recognition in Context

| 100 99 | 98 97 96 | 95 | 94 93 92 91 | 90 or less |
|---|---|---|---|---|
| Independent Level | Independent or Instructional | Instructional Level | Instructional or Frustration | Frustration Level |
| 100 95 90 | 85 80 | 75 | 70 65 60 55 | 50 or less |

Percent of Comprehension

M 1. ___ What is this story about?
(a camping trip)

F 2. ___ When did they go camping?
(Friday; after school)

F 3. ___ What was the first thing done at the campsite?
(set up a tent)

F 4. ___ Why couldn't the person go to sleep?
(he/she was eager to go trout fishing)

F 5. ___ What did they have for breakfast?
(bacon and eggs)

F 6. ___ What did the person do when awakened?
(got out of sleeping bag; got dressed and went by the fire)

I 7. ___ Who probably made the fire? Why do you think so?
(Uncle Joe)

I 8. ___ How do you think the young camper felt by the end of the day of fishing? Why do you think so?
(any logical response)

E 9. ___ How long do you think they camped? Why do you think so?
(any logical response; the weekend)

V 10. ___ What does "eager" mean?
(you really want to do something; excited)

Percent of Comprehension ____

My uncle and I went camping last week. We left home Friday after school and reached our campsite Friday night. After setting up our tent we went to bed. I could not fall asleep because I was eager to go trout fishing for the first time in my life. Finally I fell asleep only to be shaken by my uncle informing me it was time for breakfast. I got up out of my sleeping bag, got dressed, and trudged out to the blazing fire. I devoured a breakfast of bacon and eggs that Uncle Joe had prepared on the fire.

Percent of Word Recognition ____

____ WPM
$\overline{)6000}$

**Scoring Guide: Five**

Percent of Word Recognition in Context

| 100 99 | 98 97 96 | 95 | 94 93 92 91 | 90 or less |
|---|---|---|---|---|
| Independent Level | Independent or Instructional | Instructional Level | Instructional or Frustration | Frustration Level |
| 100 95 90 | 85 80 | 75 | 70 65 60 55 | 50 or less |

Percent of Comprehension

M  1. ___ What is this story about?
        (a witch and Halloween)

F  2. ___ Where did the witch live?
        (in a shady hut; in a pumpkin field)

F  3. ___ Who saw the witch?
        (no one)

F  4. ___ What was the witch's "job"?
        (to decide the fate of weather on
        Halloween Eve)

F  5. ___ Why did the witch put grape jelly
        beans in the brew?
        (to make it storm)

F  6. ___ What was seen and heard at night?
        (dim lights and odd sounds)

I  7. ___ What do you think the witch did with
        her evil brew?
        (any logical response)

I  8. ___ Was the witch's hut in good repair?
        Why?
        (any logical response)

E  9. ___ Describe how you think the inside of
        the witch's hut looked.
        (any logical response)

V  10. ___ What does "fate" mean?
        (something that happens and you can't
        do anything about it)

Percent of Comprehension ____

The heavy fog swept across a

pumpkin field where the Great Orange

Witch lived in her shady hut. At night dim

lights were seen in the cloudy windows and

odd sounds drifted out from under doors

and through cracks in the walls. No one

had ever seen the witch, but kids imagined

her to look like any other sorceress. They

were sadly mistaken. She was no ordinary

witch but one who decided the fate of

weather on Halloween Eve. If the witch

thought that it should storm on Halloween,

she would drop more grape jelly beans in

her evil brew.

Percent of Word Recognition ____

$\overline{)6000}$ WPM

## Scoring Guide:  Six

Percent of Word Recognition in Context

| 100 99 | 98 97 96 | 95 | 94 93 92 91 | 90 or less |
|--------|----------|-----|-------------|------------|
| Independent Level | Independent or Instructional | Instructional Level | Instructional or Frustration | Frustration Level |
| 100 95 90 | 85 80 | 75 | 70 65 60 55 | 50 or less |

Percent of Comprehension

M   1. ___   What is this story about?
               (a princess and her knight)

F   2. ___   How was the princess held captive?
               (she was shackled to a rock)

F   3. ___   How did the knight free the princess?
               (with his sword; he cut the chain)

F   4. ___   What did the knight do after freeing
               the princess?
               (comforted her with reassuring words;
               led her away)

F   5. ___   Who took the princess to this island?
               (the pirates)

F   6. ___   Why was the princess taken to this
               land?
               (as a peace offering to the monsters)

I   7. ___   Why do you think the pirates used her
               as a peace offering?
               (any logical response; she was
               beautiful, powerful; etc.)

I   8. ___   What do you think happened to the
               knight and the princess?
               (any logical response; they became
               friends; got married)

E   9. ___   What qualities do you think should be
               required for knighthood?
               (any logical response; bravery; courage)

V  10. ___   What does "savage" mean?
               (wild; rugged)

Percent of Comprehension ____

One of the most beloved tales is of the princess and her knight. The princess, shackled to a rock, caught the eye of the wandering knight. He galloped over and, with a single stroke of his sword, released her from the iron chain. Taking her hand, he led her away from the dreadful confinement of the rock. While relaxing in a sunny meadow, he comforted her with reassuring words. The princess told him that she had been seized by pirates. Later, she had been brought to this savage island as a peace offering to the terrible monsters of the sea.

Percent of Word Recognition ____

____ WPM
$\overline{)6000}$

## Scoring Guide: Seven

Percent of Word Recognition in Context

| 100 99 | 98 97 96 | 95 | 94 93 92 91 | 90 or less |
|---|---|---|---|---|
| Independent Level | Independent or Instructional | Instructional Level | Instructional or Frustration | Frustration Level |
| 100 95 90 | 85 80 | 75 | 70 65 60 55 | 50 or less |

Percent of Comprehension

M    1. ___    What is this story about?
(the mountain, Mt. Kilarma)

F    2. ___    How tall is Mt. Kilarma?
(15,000 feet)

F    3. ___    What are the dangers of Mt. Kilarma?
(the glaciers and changing winds at the summit)

F    4. ___    How many people had reached the summit?
(no one)

F    5. ___    On what parts of the mountain were the glaciers?
(the steep sides)

F    6. ___    What was covering the mountain?
(ice; glaciers)

I    7. ___    What do you believe the mountaineers were thinking as they stared at Mt. Kilarma?
(any logical response; whether they would be successful in the climb)

I    8. ___    What kinds of qualities do you think were present in the mountaineers? Why?
(any logical response; strength; courage; endurance)

E    9. ___    Why do you think these people would risk their lives to climb the mountain?
(any logical response; no one had ever scaled the mountain)

V    10. ___    What does "ominously" mean?
(threatening; menacing)

Percent of Comprehension _____

The mountain loomed ominously in the foreground. There it was, the lonely unconquered giant, Mt. Kilarma. In sheer size there was nothing imposing about the 15,000 foot height of Mt. Kilarma. The dangers rested in the skirt of glaciers around the steep sides of the mountain and the fiercely changing winds that tore at the summit. Many had tried to defeat this magnificent creation of nature, but to date no one had. Mindful of this, the band of mountaineers stared at the huge mass of ice. Could they reach the mountain's peak and do what no one had ever accomplished?

Percent of Word Recognition _____

_____ WPM
$\overline{)6000}$

## Scoring Guide: Eight

Percent of Word Recognition in Context

| 100 99 | 98 97 96 | 95 | 94 93 92 91 | 90 or less |
|---|---|---|---|---|
| Independent Level | Independent or Instructional | Instructional Level | Instructional or Frustration | Frustration Level |
| 100 95 90 | 85 80 | 75 | 70 65 60 55 | 50 or less |

Percent of Comprehension

# Basic Reading Inventory, Form B

Graded Word Lists
Graded Passages

| List B-B | List B | List B 1417 | List B 8224 |
|----------|--------|-------------|-------------|
| 1. we | 1. she | 1. far | 1. above |
| 2. up | 2. find | 2. may | 2. dress |
| 3. see | 3. good | 3. walk | 3. seed |
| 4. not | 4. on | 4. snow | 4. knock |
| 5. will | 5. run | 5. happy | 5. though |
| 6. get | 6. away | 6. call | 6. hear |
| 7. little | 7. like | 7. party | 7. follow |
| 8. ball | 8. home | 8. wish | 8. city |
| 9. play | 9. take | 9. apple | 9. count |
| 10. with | 10. about | 10. her | 10. bravely |
| 11. come | 11. show | 11. next | 11. across |
| 12. make | 12. all | 12. thing | 12. even |
| 13. you | 13. has | 13. could | 13. mouth |
| 14. want | 14. out | 14. back | 14. round |
| 15. in | 15. say | 15. store | 15. turn |
| 16. ride | 16. do | 16. open | 16. been |
| 17. have | 17. boy | 17. began | 17. poor |
| 18. top | 18. from | 18. live | 18. soft |
| 19. day | 19. put | 19. how | 19. front |
| 20. it | 20. he | 20. gave | 20. near |

## List B 3183

1. horn
2. noon
3. warm
4. invention
5. stove
6. fiercely
7. doctor
8. visit
9. pile
10. lift
11. thirty
12. feel
13. accident
14. mountain
15. pound
16. trap
17. ashamed
18. blizzard
19. hang
20. sight

## List B 5414

1. greet
2. mountains
3. snake
4. packet
5. disturbed
6. already
7. rescue
8. treasure
9. prepared
10. rooster
11. dozen
12. machine
13. bandit
14. trail
15. moan
16. spoon
17. beyond
18. crickets
19. condition
20. blushing

## List B 5895

1. rifle
2. honestly
3. jagged
4. silence
5. attached
6. pouches
7. turtle
8. nation
9. entrance
10. persistent
11. stream
12. bandages
13. wealthy
14. taxation
15. padded
16. increasing
17. prairie
18. beard
19. mercy
20. center

## List B 6687

1. science
2. isolate
3. customers
4. singular
5. wreath
6. pounce
7. exhausted
8. depth
9. authority
10. snowy
11. trio
12. flourish
13. procession
14. telescope
15. cease
16. knights
17. liberty
18. blond
19. medicine
20. symbol

## List B 7371

1. inquiry
2. menace
3. economists
4. socially
5. communism
6. symmetry
7. gaseous
8. amplified
9. hurdle
10. enlarge
11. thermostat
12. marveled
13. cavalry
14. beneficial
15. namely
16. boar
17. screech
18. compliment
19. mallet
20. senators

## List B 1883

1. dorsal
2. gadget
3. surgical
4. folder
5. municipal
6. sportsmanship
7. terrace
8. imperative
9. pliers
10. speculate
11. diversion
12. germinate
13. figurative
14. ransom
15. frustration
16. seizure
17. entangled
18. induction
19. saturated
20. impurities

"I cannot find my ball," said Pete. "It is a big ball. My ball is red."

"Here is a ball," Jill said. "The ball is blue. It is small. It is not red."

"I see a ball," said Pete. "It is red. It is big. It is my ball."

A white house was in the woods. Ann lived there. The sun made Ann happy. The air smelled clean. She took a walk.

Ann found something along the road in the grass. It was round and white.

"Oh!" said Ann. "What a nice egg. I'll take it home."

Mother was home.

She said, "Ann, you must keep the egg warm."

Ann filled a box with rags. She set the egg in it. She put it near the stove.

The next day Ann woke to a sound she did not know.

"Chirp." A baby chick was born. Ann had a pet.

Dan wanted to go to the zoo. He
asked mother. His mother said, "Yes."
Dan had fun at the zoo. There were many
animals he liked. One animal looked like it
had two tails. It was an elephant. One had
a nice back to ride on. It was a big turtle.
Dan looked at many things. He saw many
furry animals. He laughed at them.

Soon it was getting dark. "Where am
I?" he asked. Dan looked for his mother.
He was lost! He sat down and cried. Soon
someone moved. His mother was behind
him all the time!

B 1417

A spider sat down by Little Miss Muffet. She was afraid of it. She should not have been scared. The spider would not hurt her. Most spiders are friendly. If you think a spider is an insect, you are wrong. Spiders belong to a group of animals that have eight legs. In the fall the mother spider lays about 500 eggs. Only the strong baby spiders live. When spring comes they leave their nest. They eat flies, bugs, and ants. They also eat insects that harm our crops. You should be able to find a spider web where you live.

B 8224

The first days of the steam trains were exciting and dangerous. The trains looked like big monsters. They threw off sparks and smoke, ran off the track, and sometimes even blew up. But everyone wanted to ride these fast new steam trains. Soon trains joined the big cities in the east. Work teams blasted their way through the mountains laying tracks from the east coast to the west. New towns sprung up in places that were once prairie. When the track was finished, people rode trains from one end of the country to the other. Trains helped our country grow.

The newly built ball park was filled to capacity with happy and excited spectators. The Tigers and Jets were playing for the city championship, and the score was 10 to 9 in favor of the Jets. It was the last half of the last inning. The Tigers were up for their last time at bat. Dale, the strongest player on the team, was up first. The crowd screamed as he swung at the ball and missed. The next pitch was over the plate. Dale swung, the baseball sailed to left field into the player's glove, and the crowd went wild.

B 5414

Older airplanes were moved through the air by the use of propellers. Now, most planes are driven by large jet engines. Some fly faster than sound. The first thing you may notice about a plane is the wings that stick out on either side of its long body. Today jet planes land and take off from major airports every few seconds. People can travel around the world in only a few hours. It often takes travelers longer to retrieve their luggage than to fly to their destination. Planes have been much improved since the Wright brothers first flew in 1903.

B 5895

On our field trip we visited the new museum. We saw many different exhibits about science and the world around us. The telephone exhibit was definitely the most interesting. Phones from the early days were made of wood and metal. You had to ring the operator to make a call. There were also phones of the future. Some had televisions so that you could see the person you were talking to. They also had phones for your car that worked with a small transistor. We saw movies that showed us how the phone works for us in our everyday lives.

B 6687

The foreheads of the men glistened
with sweat as they struggled forward under
the hot sun of the tropics. These men were
guerillas who sincerely felt that their leader
was the salvation of their country. A huge
man bellowed an order from the leader as
they moved across some uninhabited land.
Their goal was to reach a distant army fort
where they hoped to fire a projectile into
the storeroom of the fort. This would cause
the gunpowder to erupt like a tinderbox.
They hoped their brave plan would scare
the soldiers and impress more local men to
join them.

B 7371

The scientist worked hard at his lab bench. He had been given a very stimulating suggestion in a letter from an unknown person. The key to success was in the radium reaction that would activate the drug he needed. From that point forward it was simply a matter of reducing the different compounds to the right one. Ultimately he would find it, and then he would have a monopoly on the drug that could make men immortal. The disappearance of death and disease would make him the most powerful person alive. Only he would know the correct amount in each dose.

B 1883

# Basic Reading Inventory: Performance Booklet
## (Form B)

*Jerry L. Johns*
*Northern Illinois University*

Student _____     Sex  M  F     Date of Testing _____

School _____ Grade _____     Date of Birth _____

Teacher _____     Examiner _____

| | SUMMARY OF STUDENT'S PERFORMANCE | | | | | | | | | | |
| --- | --- | --- | --- | --- | --- | --- | --- | --- | --- | --- | --- |
| | Word Recognition | | | | Comprehension | | | | | | Listening |
| Grade | Isolation | | Context | | Oral Reading Form A B C | | Silent Reading Form A B C | | | | Form A B C |
| | Total Score | Level | Percent Correct | Level | Percent Correct | Level | Percent Correct | Level | Rate | | Percent Correct | Level |
| PP | | | | | | | | | | | |
| P | | | | | | | | | | | |
| 1 | | | | | | | | | | | |
| 2 | | | | | | | | | | | |
| 3 | | | | | | | | | | | |
| 4 | | | | | | | | | | | |
| 5 | | | | | | | | | | | |
| 6 | | | | | | | | | | | |
| 7 | | | | | | | | | | | |
| 8 | | | | | | | | | | | |

**Estimated Levels**

Independent _____

Instructional _____

Frustration _____

Listening _____

**General Criteria for Reading Levels**

| | Ind. | Inst. | Frust. |
| --- | --- | --- | --- |
| Word Recognition (Isolation) | 19–20 | 14–18 | ≤ 13 |
| Word Recognition (Context) | 99 | 95 | 90 |
| Comprehension | 90 | 75 | 50 |

**KENDALL/HUNT PUBLISHING COMPANY**
Dubuque, Iowa

# SUMMARY OF ADMINISTRATION
## AND SCORING PROCEDURES

To determine a student's independent, instructional, and frustration levels, administer the three reading tests included in the Basic Reading Inventory as follows:

**WORD RECOGNITION IN ISOLATION:** Select a graded word list at a reading level that will be easy for the student. Ask the student to pronounce the words rapidly. Record the student's responses in the timed column beside the corresponding word list in the performance booklet.

Return to mispronounced or unknown words for a second attempt at analysis, and note the student's responses in the untimed column. Administer successive word lists until the student is no longer able to achieve a total score of at least fourteen correct words or until the student becomes frustrated.

**Scoring:** Total the correct responses in the timed and untimed columns. Consult the criteria on the general scoring guide shown below to determine the reading level achieved on each graded word list. Record the number-correct scores and the reading levels on the summary sheet of the performance booklet.

**WORD RECOGNITION IN CONTEXT:** Ask the student to read aloud the passage graded one level *below* the highest independent level achieved on the graded word lists. As the student reads the passage, record all miscues such as omissions, repetitions, substitutions, etc. on the corresponding copy of the passage found in the performance booklet.

**Scoring:** To find the percent-correct score, count the number of significant miscues (those that affect meaning) in each graded passage. At the pre-primer level, each significant miscue is valued at 2 percentage points and subtracted from 100. At the primer level and above, each significant miscue is valued at 1 percentage point and subtracted from 100.

To determine reading levels from the percent-correct scores, consult the criteria on the general scoring guide shown below. Record the percent-correct scores and the reading levels on the summary sheet of the performance booklet.

**COMPREHENSION:** Ask the comprehension questions that are beside the passage in the performance booklet and record the student's responses. Continue administering graded passages until the student has ten or more significant word recognition miscues, is unable to answer half the comprehension questions, or demonstrates behavior associated with frustration.

**Scoring:** To find the percent-correct score achieved on each passage, divide the number of correct responses by the number of questions.

To convert the percent-correct scores into reading levels, consult the criteria on the general scoring guide below. (Teacher judgment must be exercised at the pre-primer level because the limited number of questions may not permit precise measurement of achievement.) Record the percent-correct scores and the reading levels on the summary sheet of the performance booklet.

### General Scoring Guide for Reading Levels

| Subtest of Basic Reading Inventory | Independent Level | Independent or Instructional Level | Instructional Level | Instructional or Frustration Level | Frustration Level |
|---|---|---|---|---|---|
| Word Recognition in Isolation | 20–19 | | 18–14 | | 13 or less |
| Word Recognition in Context (%) | 99 | 98–96 | 95 | 94–91 | 90 or less |
| Comprehension (%) | 90 | 85–80 | 75 | 70–55 | 50 or less |

Note: Teacher judgment is necessary in gray areas.

| List B-B | Timed | Untimed | List B | Timed | Untimed |
|---|---|---|---|---|---|
| 1. we | _____ | _____ | 1. she | _____ | _____ |
| 2. up | _____ | _____ | 2. find | _____ | _____ |
| 3. see | _____ | _____ | 3. good | _____ | _____ |
| 4. not | _____ | _____ | 4. on | _____ | _____ |
| 5. will | _____ | _____ | 5. run | _____ | _____ |
| 6. get | _____ | _____ | 6. away | _____ | _____ |
| 7. little | _____ | _____ | 7. like | _____ | _____ |
| 8. ball | _____ | _____ | 8. home | _____ | _____ |
| 9. play | _____ | _____ | 9. take | _____ | _____ |
| 10. with | _____ | _____ | 10. about | _____ | _____ |
| 11. come | _____ | _____ | 11. show | _____ | _____ |
| 12. make | _____ | _____ | 12. all | _____ | _____ |
| 13. you | _____ | _____ | 13. has | _____ | _____ |
| 14. want | _____ | _____ | 14. out | _____ | _____ |
| 15. in | _____ | _____ | 15. say | _____ | _____ |
| 16. ride | _____ | _____ | 16. do | _____ | _____ |
| 17. have | _____ | _____ | 17. boy | _____ | _____ |
| 18. top | _____ | _____ | 18. from | _____ | _____ |
| 19. day | _____ | _____ | 19. put | _____ | _____ |
| 20. it | _____ | _____ | 20. he | _____ | _____ |
| Number Correct | _____ | _____ | Number Correct | _____ | _____ |
| Total Score | _____ | | Total Score | _____ | |

### Scoring Guide for Graded Word Lists

| Independent | Instructional | Frustration |
|---|---|---|
| 20 19 | 18 17 16 15 14 | 13 or less |

| List B 1417 | Timed | Untimed | List B 8224 | Timed | Untimed |
|---|---|---|---|---|---|
| 1. far | _____ | _____ | 1. above | _____ | _____ |
| 2. may | _____ | _____ | 2. dress | _____ | _____ |
| 3. walk | _____ | _____ | 3. seed | _____ | _____ |
| 4. snow | _____ | _____ | 4. knock | _____ | _____ |
| 5. happy | _____ | _____ | 5. though | _____ | _____ |
| 6. call | _____ | _____ | 6. hear | _____ | _____ |
| 7. party | _____ | _____ | 7. follow | _____ | _____ |
| 8. wish | _____ | _____ | 8. city | _____ | _____ |
| 9. apple | _____ | _____ | 9. count | _____ | _____ |
| 10. her | _____ | _____ | 10. bravely | _____ | _____ |
| 11. next | _____ | _____ | 11. across | _____ | _____ |
| 12. thing | _____ | _____ | 12. even | _____ | _____ |
| 13. could | _____ | _____ | 13. mouth | _____ | _____ |
| 14. back | _____ | _____ | 14. round | _____ | _____ |
| 15. store | _____ | _____ | 15. turn | _____ | _____ |
| 16. open | _____ | _____ | 16. been | _____ | _____ |
| 17. began | _____ | _____ | 17. poor | _____ | _____ |
| 18. live | _____ | _____ | 18. soft | _____ | _____ |
| 19. how | _____ | _____ | 19. front | _____ | _____ |
| 20. gave | _____ | _____ | 20. near | _____ | _____ |
| Number Correct | _____ | _____ | Number Correct | _____ | _____ |
| Total Score | _____ | | Total Score | _____ | |

### Scoring Guide for Graded Word Lists

| Independent | Instructional | Frustration |
|---|---|---|
| 20 19 | 18 17 16 15 14 | 13 or less |

| List B 3183 | Timed | Untimed | List B 5414 | Timed | Untimed |
|---|---|---|---|---|---|
| 1. horn | _____ | _____ | 1. greet | _____ | _____ |
| 2. noon | _____ | _____ | 2. mountains | _____ | _____ |
| 3. warm | _____ | _____ | 3. snake | _____ | _____ |
| 4. invention | _____ | _____ | 4. packet | _____ | _____ |
| 5. stove | _____ | _____ | 5. disturbed | _____ | _____ |
| 6. fiercely | _____ | _____ | 6. already | _____ | _____ |
| 7. doctor | _____ | _____ | 7. rescue | _____ | _____ |
| 8. visit | _____ | _____ | 8. treasure | _____ | _____ |
| 9. pile | _____ | _____ | 9. prepared | _____ | _____ |
| 10. lift | _____ | _____ | 10. rooster | _____ | _____ |
| 11. thirty | _____ | _____ | 11. dozen | _____ | _____ |
| 12. feel | _____ | _____ | 12. machine | _____ | _____ |
| 13. accident | _____ | _____ | 13. bandit | _____ | _____ |
| 14. mountain | _____ | _____ | 14. trail | _____ | _____ |
| 15. pound | _____ | _____ | 15. moan | _____ | _____ |
| 16. trap | _____ | _____ | 16. spoon | _____ | _____ |
| 17. ashamed | _____ | _____ | 17. beyond | _____ | _____ |
| 18. blizzard | _____ | _____ | 18. crickets | _____ | _____ |
| 19. hang | _____ | _____ | 19. condition | _____ | _____ |
| 20. sight | _____ | _____ | 20. blushing | _____ | _____ |
| Number Correct | _____ | _____ | Number Correct | _____ | _____ |
| Total Score | _____ | | Total Score | _____ | |

## Scoring Guide for Graded Word Lists

| Independent | Instructional | Frustration |
|---|---|---|
| 20 19 | 18 17 16 15 14 | 13 or less |

| List B 5895 | Timed | Untimed | List B 6687 | Timed | Untimed |
|---|---|---|---|---|---|
| 1. rifle | _____ | _____ | 1. science | _____ | _____ |
| 2. honestly | _____ | _____ | 2. isolate | _____ | _____ |
| 3. jagged | _____ | _____ | 3. customers | _____ | _____ |
| 4. silence | _____ | _____ | 4. singular | _____ | _____ |
| 5. attached | _____ | _____ | 5. wreath | _____ | _____ |
| 6. pouches | _____ | _____ | 6. pounce | _____ | _____ |
| 7. turtle | _____ | _____ | 7. exhausted | _____ | _____ |
| 8. nation | _____ | _____ | 8. depth | _____ | _____ |
| 9. entrance | _____ | _____ | 9. authority | _____ | _____ |
| 10. persistent | _____ | _____ | 10. snowy | _____ | _____ |
| 11. stream | _____ | _____ | 11. trio | _____ | _____ |
| 12. bandages | _____ | _____ | 12. flourish | _____ | _____ |
| 13. wealthy | _____ | _____ | 13. procession | _____ | _____ |
| 14. taxation | _____ | _____ | 14. telescope | _____ | _____ |
| 15. padded | _____ | _____ | 15. cease | _____ | _____ |
| 16. increasing | _____ | _____ | 16. knights | _____ | _____ |
| 17. prairie | _____ | _____ | 17. liberty | _____ | _____ |
| 18. beard | _____ | _____ | 18. blond | _____ | _____ |
| 19. mercy | _____ | _____ | 19. medicine | _____ | _____ |
| 20. center | _____ | _____ | 20. symbol | _____ | _____ |
| Number Correct | _____ | _____ | Number Correct | _____ | _____ |
| Total Score | _____ | | Total Score | _____ | |

## Scoring Guide for Graded Word Lists

| Independent | Instructional | Frustration |
|---|---|---|
| 20 19 | 18 17 16 15 14 | 13 or less |

| List B 7371 | Timed | Untimed | List B 1883 | Timed | Untimed |
|---|---|---|---|---|---|
| 1. inquiry | _____ | _____ | 1. dorsal | _____ | _____ |
| 2. menace | _____ | _____ | 2. gadget | _____ | _____ |
| 3. economists | _____ | _____ | 3. surgical | _____ | _____ |
| 4. socially | _____ | _____ | 4. folder | _____ | _____ |
| 5. communism | _____ | _____ | 5. municipal | _____ | _____ |
| 6. symmetry | _____ | _____ | 6. sportsmanship | _____ | _____ |
| 7. gaseous | _____ | _____ | 7. terrace | _____ | _____ |
| 8. amplified | _____ | _____ | 8. imperative | _____ | _____ |
| 9. hurdle | _____ | _____ | 9. pliers | _____ | _____ |
| 10. enlarge | _____ | _____ | 10. speculate | _____ | _____ |
| 11. thermostat | _____ | _____ | 11. diversion | _____ | _____ |
| 12. marveled | _____ | _____ | 12. germinate | _____ | _____ |
| 13. cavalry | _____ | _____ | 13. figurative | _____ | _____ |
| 14. beneficial | _____ | _____ | 14. ransom | _____ | _____ |
| 15. namely | _____ | _____ | 15. frustration | _____ | _____ |
| 16. boar | _____ | _____ | 16. seizure | _____ | _____ |
| 17. screech | _____ | _____ | 17. entangled | _____ | _____ |
| 18. compliment | _____ | _____ | 18. induction | _____ | _____ |
| 19. mallet | _____ | _____ | 19. saturated | _____ | _____ |
| 20. senators | _____ | _____ | 20. impurities | _____ | _____ |

Number Correct _____ _____     Number Correct _____ _____

Total Score _____     Total Score _____

### Scoring Guide for Graded Word Lists

| Independent | Instructional | Frustration |
|---|---|---|
| 20 19 | 18 17 16 15 14 | 13 or less |

91

F    1. ___ What happened to Pete?
(he lost his ball)

F    2. ___ What did the ball Jill found look like?
(blue and small)

E    3. ___ How do you think Pete lost his ball?
(any logical response)

I    4. ___ How did Pete know that the ball Jill found wasn't his?
(any logical response; it was small and blue)

V    5. ___ What does "find" mean?
(to locate; to look for something and then see it)

"I cannot find my ball," said Pete. "It is a big ball. My ball is red."

"Here is a ball," Jill said. "The ball is blue. It is small. It is not red."

"I see a ball," said Pete. "It is red. It is big. It is my ball."

Percent of Word Recognition ____

____ WPM
)3000

Percent of Comprehension ____

## Scoring Guide: Pre-Primer

Percent of Word Recognition in Context

| 100 99 | 98 97 96 | 95 | 94 93 92 91 | 90 or less |
|--------|----------|----|----|------------|
| Independent Level | Independent or Instructional | Instructional Level | Instructional or Frustration | Frustration Level |
| 100 95 90 | 85 80 | 75 | 70 65 60 55 | 50 or less |

Percent of Comprehension

**B**

| | | | |
|---|---|---|---|
| M | 1. ___ | What is this story about? (a girl named Ann who found an egg that hatched) | |

A white house was in the woods. Ann lived there. The sun made Ann happy. The air smelled clean. She took a walk.

F    2. ___ Where did Ann live? (in the woods; in a white house)

Ann found something along the road in the grass. It was round and white.

F    3. ___ What was the air like in the woods? (it smelled clean)

"Oh!" said Ann. "What a nice egg. I'll take it home."

F    4. ___ What happened to Ann? (she went on a walk; she found an egg)

Mother was home.

F    5. ___ Where did Ann find the egg? (along the road in the grass)

She said, "Ann, you must keep the egg warm."

F    6. ___ What did Ann do to make the egg hatch? (put it near the stove in a box)

Ann filled a box with rags. She set the egg in it. She put it near the stove.

I    7. ___ How do you think the egg got in the grass along the road? (any logical response)

The next day Ann woke to a sound she did not know.

I    8. ___ Why was it important to keep the egg warm? (any logical response; so it would hatch)

"Chirp." A baby chick was born. Ann had a pet.

E    9. ___ What other things might Ann have found on her walk? (any logical response; tracks, leaves, rocks, etc.)

Percent of Word Recognition ____

V    10. ___ What is a "pet"? (an animal to love, play with, etc.)

____ WPM
)6000

Percent of Comprehension ____

### Scoring Guide: Primer
Percent of Word Recognition in Context

| 100 99 | 98 97 96 | 95 | 94 93 92 91 | 90 or less |
|---|---|---|---|---|
| Independent Level | Independent or Instructional | Instructional Level | Instructional or Frustration | Frustration Level |
| 100 95 90 | 85 80 | 75 | 70 65 60 55 | 50 or less |

Percent of Comprehension

93

M 1. ___ What is this story about?
(a boy's trip to the zoo)

F 2. ___ Who did he ask?
(his mother)

F 3. ___ What did Dan think he could do with the turtle?
(ride it)

F 4. ___ What other types of animals did Dan see at the zoo?
(furry animals; elephant)

F 5. ___ How did Dan think the elephant looked?
(like it had two tails)

F 6. ___ Where was Dan's mother when he was lost?
(behind him)

I 7. ___ Why do you think Dan wanted to go to the zoo?
(any logical response)

I 8. ___ Why do you think Dan cried?
(any logical response; he was scared)

E 9. ___ What do you think the animals did to make Dan laugh?
(any logical response)

V 10. ___ What does "furry" mean?
(covered with fur; soft)

Percent of Comprehension ____

Dan wanted to go to the zoo. He asked mother. His mother said, "Yes." Dan had fun at the zoo. There were many animals he liked. One animal looked like it had two tails. It was an elephant. One had a nice back to ride on. It was a big turtle. Dan looked at many things. He saw many furry animals. He laughed at them.

Soon it was getting dark. "Where am I?" he asked. Dan looked for his mother. He was lost! He sat down and cried. Soon someone moved. His mother was behind him all the time!

Percent of Word Recognition ____

$\overline{\phantom{WPM}}$ WPM
$)\overline{6000}$

### Scoring Guide: One

Percent of Word Recognition in Context

| 100 99 | 98 97 96 | 95 | 94 93 92 91 | 90 or less |
|---|---|---|---|---|
| Independent Level | Independent or Instructional | Instructional Level | Instructional or Frustration | Frustration Level |
| 100 95 90 | 85 80 | 75 | 70 65 60 55 | 50 or less |

Percent of Comprehension

**B 8224**

M 1. ___ What is this story about?
(spiders)

F 2. ___ What did the spider do in this story?
(sat by Little Miss Muffet)

F 3. ___ How many legs does a spider have?
(eight)

F 4. ___ What do spiders eat?
(flies, bugs, and ants [any two])

F 5. ___ When do mother spiders lay their eggs?
(fall)

F 6. ___ How many eggs does a mother spider lay?
(500)

I 7. ___ How do most spiders catch their food?
(in their webs)

I 8. ___ What happens to weak baby spiders?
(any logical response; they die)

E 9. ___ Why do you think some people are afraid of spiders?
(any logical response)

V 10. ___ What is an "insect"?
(any logical response)

Percent of Comprehension ____

A spider sat down by Little Miss Muffet. She was afraid of it. She should not have been scared. The spider would not hurt her. Most spiders are friendly. If you think a spider is an insect, you are wrong. Spiders belong to a group of animals that have eight legs. In the fall the mother spider lays about 500 eggs. Only the strong baby spiders live. When spring comes they leave their nest. They eat flies, bugs, and ants. They also eat insects that harm our crops. You should be able to find a spider web where you live.

Percent of Word Recognition ____

____ WPM
$\overline{)6000}$

## Scoring Guide: Two
### Percent of Word Recognition in Context

| 100 99 | 98 97 96 | 95 | 94 93 92 91 | 90 or less |
|---|---|---|---|---|
| Independent Level | Independent or Instructional | Instructional Level | Instructional or Frustration | Frustration Level |
| 100 95 90 | 85 80 | 75 | 70 65 60 55 | 50 or less |

### Percent of Comprehension

M 1. ___ What is this story about?
(early trains and things that happened to them)

F 2. ___ What did the trains look like?
(big monsters)

F 3. ___ What kind of trains is this story about?
(steam trains; early trains)

F 4. ___ What sometimes happened to the trains?
(they threw off sparks and smoke; they ran off the track; they blew up)

F 5. ___ How did the work teams get through the mountains?
(by blasting)

F 6. ___ What happened on the prairies?
(towns sprung up)

I 7. ___ How did trains help our country grow?
(any logical response; they linked cities)

I 8. ___ Why do you think people wanted to ride the steam trains?
(any logical response; they were new; they were exciting)

E 9. ___ What dangers do you think the work teams had in laying the track?
(any logical response; injuries and death)

V 10. ___ What is a "prairie"?
(grassland; land without many trees)

The first days of the steam trains were exciting and dangerous. The trains looked like big monsters. They threw off sparks and smoke, ran off the track, and sometimes even blew up. But everyone wanted to ride these fast new steam trains. Soon trains joined the big cities in the east. Work teams blasted their way through the mountains laying tracks from the east coast to the west. New towns sprung up in places that were once prairie. When the track was finished, people rode trains from one end of the country to the other. Trains helped our country grow.

Percent of Word Recognition ___

___ WPM
$)\overline{6000}$

Percent of Comprehension ___

## Scoring Guide: Three

Percent of Word Recognition in Context

| 100 99 | 98 97 96 | 95 | 94 93 92 91 | 90 or less |
|---|---|---|---|---|
| Independent Level | Independent or Instructional | Instructional Level | Instructional or Frustration | Frustration Level |
| 100 95 90 | 85 80 | 75 | 70 65 60 55 | 50 or less |

Percent of Comprehension

**B 5414**

M   1. ___ What is this story about?
(a ball game)

F   2. ___ Why was the ball park so packed with spectators?
(it was the championship game)

F   3. ___ What was the score and who was winning?
(ten to nine in favor of the Jets)

F   4. ___ What inning was it?
(it was the last inning)

F   5. ___ Who was the strongest hitter for the Tigers?
(Dale)

F   6. ___ What happened to the ball Dale hit?
(the left fielder caught it)

I   7. ___ Why do you think the crowd went wild?
(any logical response)

I   8. ___ How do you think Dale felt after he hit the ball?
(any logical response)

E   9. ___ Who do you think won the game? Why?
(any logical response)

V   10. ___ What are "spectators"?
(people who watch a ball game; they sit in the stands)

The newly built ball park was filled to capacity with happy and excited spectators. The Tigers and Jets were playing for the city championship, and the score was 10 to 9 in favor of the Jets. It was the last half of the last inning. The Tigers were up for their last time at bat. Dale, the strongest player on the team, was up first. The crowd screamed as he swung at the ball and missed. The next pitch was over the plate. Dale swung, the baseball sailed to left field into the player's glove, and the crowd went wild.

Percent of Word Recognition _____

_____ WPM
$6000$

Percent of Comprehension _____

## Scoring Guide: Four
Percent of Word Recognition in Context

| 100 99 | 98 97 96 | 95 | 94 93 92 91 | 90 or less |
|---|---|---|---|---|
| Independent Level | Independent or Instructional | Instructional Level | Instructional or Frustration | Frustration Level |
| 100 95 90 | 85 80 | 75 | 70 65 60 55 | 50 or less |

Percent of Comprehension

M   1. \_\_\_ What is this story about?
(planes; the progressive development of planes through the years)

F   2. \_\_\_ What kind of engines do most airplanes have today?
(jet engines)

F   3. \_\_\_ How were older planes moved through the air?
(propellers)

F   4. \_\_\_ In what year did the Wright brothers fly?
(1903)

F   5. \_\_\_ According to this story, what is the first thing you will probably notice about an airplane?
(the wings that stick out from the body of the plane)

F   6. \_\_\_ How often do airplanes take off and land from major airports?
(every few seconds)

I   7. \_\_\_ Do you think the planes of today are safer than early planes? Why?
(any logical response)

I   8. \_\_\_ Why might a jet engine plane be better than a propeller engine plane?
(any logical response)

E   9. \_\_\_ How do you think jet airplanes have changed our lives?
(any logical response)

V  10. \_\_\_ What is a "destination"?
(a place you are trying to get to)

Percent of Comprehension \_\_\_\_

Older airplanes were moved through the air by the use of propellers. Now, most planes are driven by large jet engines. Some fly faster than sound. The first thing you may notice about a plane is the wings that stick out on either side of its long body. Today jet planes land and take off from major airports every few seconds. People can travel around the world in only a few hours. It often takes travelers longer to retrieve their luggage than to fly to their destination. Planes have been much improved since the Wright brothers first flew in 1903.

Percent of Word Recognition \_\_\_\_

$\dfrac{\phantom{xxxx}}{\smash{)6000}}$ WPM

## Scoring Guide: Five

Percent of Word Recognition in Context

| 100 99 | 98 97 96 | 95 | 94 93 92 91 | 90 or less |
|---|---|---|---|---|
| Independent Level | Independent or Instructional | Instructional Level | Instructional or Frustration | Frustration Level |
| 100 95 90 | 85 80 | 75 | 70 65 60 55 | 50 or less |

Percent of Comprehension

**B 6687**

M    1. ___   What is the story about?
             (a field trip to the museum; a telephone
             exhibit)

F    2. ___   What were some of the exhibits?
             (science; telephone; world around us
             [any two])

F    3. ___   What materials were used to make the
             early phones?
             (wood and metal)

F    4. ___   What did you have to do to make a
             phone call with early phones?
             (call the operator)

F    5. ___   What are the phones of the future like?
             (they have televisions)

F    6. ___   How do phones in cars work?
             (with a small transistor)

I    7. ___   Do you think our phones are better
             than the early phones? Why?
             (any logical response; can dial a call)

I    8. ___   Why do you think seeing the person
             you are talking to on television might
             be a good idea?
             (any logical response)

E    9. ___   Do you think telephones have made our
             lives better? Why?
             (any logical response)

V    10. ___   What is an "exhibit"?
             (any logical response; a display of
             objects)

Percent of Comprehension ___

On our field trip we visited the new museum. We saw many different exhibits about science and the world around us. The telephone exhibit was definitely the most interesting. Phones from the early days were made of wood and metal. You had to ring the operator to make a call. There were also phones of the future. Some had televisions so that you could see the person you were talking to. They also had phones for your car that worked with a small transistor. We saw movies that showed us how the phone works for us in our everyday lives.

Percent of Word Recognition ___

___ WPM
)6000

**Scoring Guide: Six**

Percent of Word Recognition in Context

| 100 99 | 98 97 96 | 95 | 94 93 92 91 | 90 or less |
|---|---|---|---|---|
| Independent Level | Independent or Instructional | Instructional Level | Instructional or Frustration | Frustration Level |
| 100 95 90 | 85 80 | 75 | 70 65 60 55 | 50 or less |

Percent of Comprehension

M    1. ___   What is the main idea of this story?
                (a guerilla raid on an army fort; life
                among guerilla fighters)

F    2. ___   What was the weather like?
                (hot tropical sunshine)

F    3. ___   How did the men feel about their
                leader?
                (they felt he was the salvation of their
                country)

F    4. ___   What kind of land were they traveling
                in?
                (uninhabited; tropics)

F    5. ___   What was the guerillas' plan?
                (to destroy the gunpowder of the army
                fort)

F    6. ___   What did they hope to accomplish?
                (scare soldiers; impress local men to
                join them)

I    7. ___   Why do you think the guerillas wanted
                to scare the soldiers?
                (any logical response)

I    8. ___   What do you think the soldiers will do
                if the guerillas succeed?
                (any logical response)

E    9. ___   What dangers do you think might be
                involved for the guerillas in their
                attack?
                (any logical response)

V   10. ___   What does "glistened" mean?
                (to shine; to stand out)

Percent of Comprehension ____

The foreheads of the men glistened with sweat as they struggled forward under the hot sun of the tropics. These men were guerillas who sincerely felt that their leader was the salvation of their country. A huge man bellowed an order from the leader as they moved across some uninhabited land. Their goal was to reach a distant army fort where they hoped to fire a projectile into the storeroom of the fort. This would cause the gunpowder to erupt like a tinderbox. They hoped their brave plan would scare the soldiers and impress more local men to join them.

Percent of Word Recognition ____

_____ WPM
) 6000

## Scoring Guide:  Seven

Percent of Word Recognition in Context

| 100 99 | 98 97 96 | 95 | 94 93 92 91 | 90 or less |
|---|---|---|---|---|
| Independent Level | Independent or Instructional | Instructional Level | Instructional or Frustration | Frustration Level |
| 100 95 90 | 85 80 | 75 | 70 65 60 55 | 50 or less |

Percent of Comprehension

M   1. ___   What is the main idea of this story?
(a scientist is searching for a drug to make men immortal)

F   2. ___   Where did the scientist get the idea for the formula?
(in a letter from an unknown person)

F   3. ___   What was the key to the experiment?
(the radium reaction)

F   4. ___   What would the radium reaction do?
(activate the drug he needed)

F   5. ___   What would the drug eliminate?
(death and disease [any one])

F   6. ___   Why would the scientist be powerful?
(only he would know the right amount in each dose)

I   7. ___   How do you think people would react to this discovery?
(any logical response)

I   8. ___   Do you think the scientist would be placing himself in a dangerous position? Why?
(any logical response)

E   9. ___   Would you like to be this scientist? Why?
(any logical response)

V   10. ___   What does "immortal" mean?
(to live forever; not to die)

Percent of Comprehension ____

The scientist worked hard at his lab bench. He had been given a very stimulating suggestion in a letter from an unknown person. The key to success was in the radium reaction that would activate the drug he needed. From that point forward it was simply a matter of reducing the different compounds to the right one. Ultimately he would find it, and then he would have a monopoly on the drug that could make men immortal. The disappearance of death and disease would make him the most powerful person alive. Only he would know the correct amount in each dose.

Percent of Word Recognition ____

____ WPM
) 6000

### Scoring Guide: Eight
Percent of Word Recognition in Context

| 100 99 | 98 97 96 | 95 | 94 93 92 91 | 90 or less |
|---|---|---|---|---|
| Independent Level | Independent or Instructional | Instructional Level | Instructional or Frustration | Frustration Level |
| 100 95 90 | 85 80 | 75 | 70 65 60 55 | 50 or less |

Percent of Comprehension

# Basic Reading Inventory, Form C

Graded Word Lists
Graded Passages

| List C-C | List C | List C 1417 | List C 8224 |
|----------|--------|-------------|-------------|
| 1. down | 1. father | 1. morning | 1. through |
| 2. work | 2. saw | 2. picture | 2. parade |
| 3. fast | 3. now | 3. sing | 3. gray |
| 4. no | 4. word | 4. does | 4. silver |
| 5. to | 5. know | 5. had | 5. blew |
| 6. dog | 6. one | 6. way | 6. wave |
| 7. big | 7. around | 7. coat | 7. feed |
| 8. who | 8. goat | 8. baby | 8. ten |
| 9. green | 9. thank | 9. fight | 9. real |
| 10. funny | 10. too | 10. ready | 10. chase |
| 11. said | 11. man | 11. or | 11. track |
| 12. this | 12. house | 12. pocket | 12. winter |
| 13. did | 13. car | 13. truck | 13. joke |
| 14. can | 14. him | 14. bee | 14. star |
| 15. are | 15. bike | 15. made | 15. done |
| 16. want | 16. of | 16. street | 16. such |
| 17. me | 17. should | 17. school | 17. different |
| 18. help | 18. book | 18. it's | 18. splash |
| 19. stop | 19. pet | 19. brown | 19. shirt |
| 20. ran | 20. some | 20. friend | 20. meet |

### List C 3183

1. surround
2. mama
3. customer
4. pilot
5. yesterday
6. fault
7. drew
8. spent
9. buckskin
10. gaze
11. rule
12. jungle
13. beach
14. valley
15. net
16. history
17. chuckle
18. tight
19. pump
20. shot

### List C 5414

1. factory
2. opposite
3. unexpected
4. receive
5. gym
6. plod
7. wooden
8. hunger
9. distant
10. author
11. moccasin
12. boss
13. scar
14. legend
15. starve
16. tend
17. choice
18. sleeve
19. cot
20. friendship

### List C 5895

1. celebration
2. severe
3. husky
4. graduate
5. wept
6. soothing
7. nightmare
8. kit
9. towel
10. employ
11. petal
12. mask
13. constitution
14. astounded
15. sullen
16. public
17. bleed
18. flank
19. rib
20. determination

### List C 6687

1. shrunk
2. mammoth
3. overlook
4. contribute
5. python
6. assembly
7. fanatical
8. location
9. turf
10. gallery
11. riot
12. plume
13. inquire
14. headlong
15. blister
16. technician
17. sprint
18. civilization
19. definite
20. dwelt

### List C 7371

1. furtive
2. confidential
3. rogue
4. vetoed
5. barometer
6. armament
7. exploit
8. attain
9. rehearse
10. theoretical
11. potential
12. cremation
13. mystic
14. trudge
15. pulp
16. fickle
17. subside
18. institution
19. diverge
20. fundamental

### List C 1883

1. charitable
2. optimism
3. rudimentary
4. hearsay
5. specialist
6. rebuke
7. absolute
8. intermittent
9. precipitation
10. residue
11. asphalt
12. dishonorable
13. martial
14. chronological
15. phantom
16. ardent
17. congested
18. imploringly
19. obsolete
20. remote

"Here it comes!" said Tom.

"I can see it," said Beth. "Here comes the band!"

Tom jumped up and down. "Look at the man. He is funny. I can see his red hat."

"Look!" said Beth. "I see a dog. Here comes a car. It is big. This is fun!"

"See the small birds," said Jim. "They are looking in the snow. They want food."

"The snow is deep," said Meg. "They cannot find food."

Jim said, "Let's help them."

"Yes," said Meg. "We can get bread for them."

Jim and Meg ran home. They asked Mother for bread. Mother gave bread to them. Then they ran to find the birds.

"There are the birds," said Meg. "Give them the bread."

Jim put the bread on the snow.

Meg said, "Look at the birds! They are eating the bread."

"They are happy now," said Jim. "They are fat and happy."

C

Bill had many leaves in his yard. Bill raked them into a big pile. Pat helped.

Then Bill got a very good idea.
He ran and jumped in that pile of leaves.

"Wow! What fun!"

"Let me jump," said Pat. So he jumped in too.

Soon both boys were diving in. They threw leaves into the air.

Mother looked out and said, "I see two boys having fun. Do I hear only *two* boys?"

"See our big pile!" said Bill.

"Where?" asked Mother.

The boys looked around. The pile was not big now. The leaves were all over the yard.

C 1417

Bob works at the zoo. He takes care of all kinds of animals. The animals are brought to the zoo from all over the world. Bob gives hay to the elephant. He feeds raw meat to the lion and fresh fish to the seal. He knows just what to give every animal. Each day Bob washes the cages in the zoo. When an animal gets sick, Bob takes it to the zoo doctor. He will make it well. Bob keeps the zoo keys. When the people go home, Bob locks the gates to the zoo. Then he can go home.

Sally really wanted a little dog. One day she went with her parents to the pet shop. They looked at the fish, turtles, canaries, cats, and, of course, dogs. Sally and her parents saw one nice puppy that acted very lively. It looked like a small bouncing black ball of fur. The puppy was a fluffy black poodle. It jumped around in its cage. When Sally petted the puppy, it sat up and begged. Sally and her parents laughed because the poodle looked so cute. They decided to buy the poodle. After all, who could resist such a smart dog?

The summer had been a dry one, unusual for this area. Trees and bushes in the forest wilted and died. One afternoon it began to rain. A storm descended upon the forest. Thunder and lightning were heard and seen in the forest. Suddenly a spark touched the dry leaves and a fire began. The animals warned each other as they hurried to escape the flames. As the fire came closer, trees fell to the ground. Their branches were yellow and red. The smoke was so thick the animals could hardly breathe. Many could not escape the danger of the flames.

When the first settlers came to America, there were no special men to build houses, so they did the work themselves. All the people in the area would come and help. Some men would cut the trees and others would take this wood and start forming the frame of the house. The work was tedious and long and gave the men enormous appetites. Feeding them was the women's work. They brought large quantities of food and set it outside on long wooden tables. The older children assisted by carting bits of wood or helping the women. The younger children played.

C 5895

Among the most amazing flowers found in the Midwest is the sunflower. Legend states that the flower got its name from its strange habit of turning its head in order to face the sun all day. The sunflower is a very strong plant ranging in height from three to fifteen feet. The head of the sunflower is like that of the daisy. Both have an outer circle of wide yellow petals and an inner circle of small brown flowers. Seeds later form from these small flowers. These seeds produce some of the most unique patterns found in the plant world.

Indians worshipped the power in natural things, such as the stars, moon, and the sun. At various times during the year they would hold festivals in honor of this power that they named the Great Spirit. On those occasions they would have ceremonies of dancing and feasting. The braves would decorate their bodies and faces and dress themselves in their best clothes. A medicine man would lead them in the celebration that continued for several days. While gathered about the council fire, the braves prayed that the Great Spirit would reveal his wish for them by sending some sign.

C 7371

Besides using plants and animals for food, man uses the hides of animals for shoes, the wood from trees to build houses, the fiber from the cotton plant to make his shirts, and the wool from sheep to make his suits and coats. Even the synthetic fibers that man uses are made from matter found in the environment.

Man and his environment are interdependent, but that is not the whole story. Modern man can do much more; he uses science and technology to change his environment. Because of his brain, man can investigate his environment and sometimes change it.

C 1883

# Basic Reading Inventory: Performance Booklet
## (Form C)

*Jerry L. Johns*
*Northern Illinois University*

Student _____    Sex  M  F    Date of Testing _____

School _____ Grade _____    Date of Birth _____

Teacher _____    Examiner _____

| | SUMMARY OF STUDENT'S PERFORMANCE | | | | | | | | | | |
|---|---|---|---|---|---|---|---|---|---|---|---|
| | **Word Recognition** | | | | **Comprehension** | | | | | | **Listening** |
| **Grade** | **Isolation** | | **Context** | | **Oral Reading** Form A B C | | **Silent Reading** Form A B C | | | | **Form A B C** |
| | Total Score | Level | Percent Correct | Level | Percent Correct | Level | Percent Correct | Level | Rate | | Percent Correct | Level |
| PP | | | | | | | | | | | |
| P | | | | | | | | | | | |
| 1 | | | | | | | | | | | |
| 2 | | | | | | | | | | | |
| 3 | | | | | | | | | | | |
| 4 | | | | | | | | | | | |
| 5 | | | | | | | | | | | |
| 6 | | | | | | | | | | | |
| 7 | | | | | | | | | | | |
| 8 | | | | | | | | | | | |

**Estimated Levels**

Independent _____

Instructional _____

Frustration _____

Listening _____

**General Criteria for Reading Levels**

| | *Ind.* | *Inst.* | *Frust.* |
|---|---|---|---|
| Word Recognition (Isolation) | 19–20 | 14–18 | ≤ 13 |
| Word Recognition (Context) | 99 | 95 | 90 |
| Comprehension | 90 | 75 | 50 |

**K|H**

**KENDALL/HUNT PUBLISHING COMPANY**
Dubuque, Iowa

# SUMMARY OF ADMINISTRATION
## AND SCORING PROCEDURES

To determine a student's independent, instructional, and frustration levels, administer the three reading tests included in the Basic Reading Inventory as follows:

**WORD RECOGNITION IN ISOLATION:** Select a graded word list at a reading level that will be easy for the student. Ask the student to pronounce the words rapidly. Record the student's responses in the timed column beside the corresponding word list in the performance booklet.

Return to mispronounced or unknown words for a second attempt at analysis, and note the student's responses in the untimed column. Administer successive word lists until the student is no longer able to achieve a total score of at least fourteen correct words or until the student becomes frustrated.

**Scoring:** Total the correct responses in the timed and untimed columns. Consult the criteria on the general scoring guide shown below to determine the reading level achieved on each graded word list. Record the number-correct scores and the reading levels on the summary sheet of the performance booklet.

**WORD RECOGNITION IN CONTEXT:** Ask the student to read aloud the passage graded one level *below* the highest independent level achieved on the graded word lists. As the student reads the passage, record all miscues such as omissions, repetitions, substitutions, etc. on the corresponding copy of the passage found in the performance booklet.

**Scoring:** To find the percent-correct score, count the number of significant miscues (those that affect meaning) in each graded passage. At the pre-primer level, each significant miscue is valued at 2 percentage points and subtracted from 100. At the primer level and above, each significant miscue is valued at 1 percentage point and subtracted from 100.

To determine reading levels from the percent-correct scores, consult the criteria on the general scoring guide shown below. Record the percent-correct scores and the reading levels on the summary sheet of the performance booklet.

**COMPREHENSION:** Ask the comprehension questions that are beside the passage in the performance booklet and record the student's responses. Continue administering graded passages until the student has ten or more significant word recognition miscues, is unable to answer half the comprehension questions, or demonstrates behavior associated with frustration.

**Scoring:** To find the percent-correct score achieved on each passage, divide the number of correct responses by the number of questions.

To convert the percent-correct scores into reading levels, consult the criteria on the general scoring guide below. (Teacher judgment must be exercised at the pre-primer level because the limited number of questions may not permit precise measurement of achievement.) Record the percent-correct scores and the reading levels on the summary sheet of the performance booklet.

### General Scoring Guide for Reading Levels

| Subtest of Basic Reading Inventory | Independent Level | Independent or Instructional Level | Instructional Level | Instructional or Frustration Level | Frustration Level |
|---|---|---|---|---|---|
| Word Recognition in Isolation | 20–19 | | 18–14 | | 13 or less |
| Word Recognition in Context (%) | 99 | 98–96 | 95 | 94–91 | 90 or less |
| Comprehension (%) | 90 | 85–80 | 75 | 70–55 | 50 or less |

Note: Teacher judgment is necessary in gray areas.

| List C-C | Timed | Untimed | List C | Timed | Untimed |
|---|---|---|---|---|---|
| 1. down | ____ | ____ | 1. father | ____ | ____ |
| 2. work | ____ | ____ | 2. saw | ____ | ____ |
| 3. fast | ____ | ____ | 3. now | ____ | ____ |
| 4. no | ____ | ____ | 4. word | ____ | ____ |
| 5. to | ____ | ____ | 5. know | ____ | ____ |
| 6. dog | ____ | ____ | 6. one | ____ | ____ |
| 7. big | ____ | ____ | 7. around | ____ | ____ |
| 8. who | ____ | ____ | 8. goat | ____ | ____ |
| 9. green | ____ | ____ | 9. thank | ____ | ____ |
| 10. funny | ____ | ____ | 10. too | ____ | ____ |
| 11. said | ____ | ____ | 11. man | ____ | ____ |
| 12. this | ____ | ____ | 12. house | ____ | ____ |
| 13. did | ____ | ____ | 13. car | ____ | ____ |
| 14. can | ____ | ____ | 14. him | ____ | ____ |
| 15. are | ____ | ____ | 15. bike | ____ | ____ |
| 16. want | ____ | ____ | 16. of | ____ | ____ |
| 17. me | ____ | ____ | 17. should | ____ | ____ |
| 18. help | ____ | ____ | 18. book | ____ | ____ |
| 19. stop | ____ | ____ | 19. pet | ____ | ____ |
| 20. ran | ____ | ____ | 20. some | ____ | ____ |

Number Correct ____ ____  Number Correct ____ ____

Total Score ____  Total Score ____

## Scoring Guide for Graded Word Lists

| Independent | Instructional | Frustration |
|---|---|---|
| 20 19 | 18 17 16 15 14 | 13 or less |

| List C 1417 | Timed | Untimed | List C 8224 | Timed | Untimed |
|---|---|---|---|---|---|
| 1. morning | _____ | _____ | 1. through | _____ | _____ |
| 2. picture | _____ | _____ | 2. parade | _____ | _____ |
| 3. sing | _____ | _____ | 3. gray | _____ | _____ |
| 4. does | _____ | _____ | 4. silver | _____ | _____ |
| 5. had | _____ | _____ | 5. blew | _____ | _____ |
| 6. way | _____ | _____ | 6. wave | _____ | _____ |
| 7. coat | _____ | _____ | 7. feed | _____ | _____ |
| 8. baby | _____ | _____ | 8. ten | _____ | _____ |
| 9. fight | _____ | _____ | 9. real | _____ | _____ |
| 10. ready | _____ | _____ | 10. chase | _____ | _____ |
| 11. or | _____ | _____ | 11. track | _____ | _____ |
| 12. pocket | _____ | _____ | 12. winter | _____ | _____ |
| 13. truck | _____ | _____ | 13. joke | _____ | _____ |
| 14. bee | _____ | _____ | 14. star | _____ | _____ |
| 15. made | _____ | _____ | 15. done | _____ | _____ |
| 16. street | _____ | _____ | 16. such | _____ | _____ |
| 17. school | _____ | _____ | 17. different | _____ | _____ |
| 18. it's | _____ | _____ | 18. splash | _____ | _____ |
| 19. brown | _____ | _____ | 19. shirt | _____ | _____ |
| 20. friend | _____ | _____ | 20. meet | _____ | _____ |
| Number Correct | _____ | _____ | Number Correct | _____ | _____ |
| Total Score | | _____ | Total Score | | _____ |

## Scoring Guide for Graded Word Lists

| Independent | Instructional | Frustration |
|---|---|---|
| 20 19 | 18 17 16 15 14 | 13 or less |

| List C 3183 | Timed | Untimed | List C 5414 | Timed | Untimed |
|---|---|---|---|---|---|
| 1. surround | | | 1. factory | | |
| 2. mama | | | 2. opposite | | |
| 3. customer | | | 3. unexpected | | |
| 4. pilot | | | 4. receive | | |
| 5. yesterday | | | 5. gym | | |
| 6. fault | | | 6. plod | | |
| 7. drew | | | 7. wooden | | |
| 8. spent | | | 8. hunger | | |
| 9. buckskin | | | 9. distant | | |
| 10. gaze | | | 10. author | | |
| 11. rule | | | 11. moccasin | | |
| 12. jungle | | | 12. boss | | |
| 13. beach | | | 13. scar | | |
| 14. valley | | | 14. legend | | |
| 15. net | | | 15. starve | | |
| 16. history | | | 16. tend | | |
| 17. chuckle | | | 17. choice | | |
| 18. tight | | | 18. sleeve | | |
| 19. pump | | | 19. cot | | |
| 20. shot | | | 20. friendship | | |
| Number Correct | | | Number Correct | | |
| Total Score | | | Total Score | | |

**Scoring Guide for Graded Word Lists**

| Independent | Instructional | Frustration |
|---|---|---|
| 20 19 | 18 17 16 15 14 | 13 or less |

| List C 5895 | Timed | Untimed | List C 6687 | Timed | Untimed |
|---|---|---|---|---|---|
| 1. celebration | | | 1. shrunk | | |
| 2. severe | | | 2. mammoth | | |
| 3. husky | | | 3. overlook | | |
| 4. graduate | | | 4. contribute | | |
| 5. wept | | | 5. python | | |
| 6. soothing | | | 6. assembly | | |
| 7. nightmare | | | 7. fanatical | | |
| 8. kit | | | 8. location | | |
| 9. towel | | | 9. turf | | |
| 10. employ | | | 10. gallery | | |
| 11. petal | | | 11. riot | | |
| 12. mask | | | 12. plume | | |
| 13. constitution | | | 13. inquire | | |
| 14. astounded | | | 14. headlong | | |
| 15. sullen | | | 15. blister | | |
| 16. public | | | 16. technician | | |
| 17. bleed | | | 17. sprint | | |
| 18. flank | | | 18. civilization | | |
| 19. rib | | | 19. definite | | |
| 20. determination | | | 20. dwelt | | |

Number Correct _____  _____

Total Score _____

Number Correct _____  _____

Total Score _____

## Scoring Guide for Graded Word Lists

| Independent | Instructional | Frustration |
|---|---|---|
| 20 19 | 18 17 16 15 14 | 13 or less |

| List C 7371 | Timed | Untimed | List C 1883 | Timed | Untimed |
|---|---|---|---|---|---|
| 1. furtive | _____ | _____ | 1. charitable | _____ | _____ |
| 2. confidential | _____ | _____ | 2. optimism | _____ | _____ |
| 3. rogue | _____ | _____ | 3. rudimentary | _____ | _____ |
| 4. vetoed | _____ | _____ | 4. hearsay | _____ | _____ |
| 5. barometer | _____ | _____ | 5. specialist | _____ | _____ |
| 6. armament | _____ | _____ | 6. rebuke | _____ | _____ |
| 7. exploit | _____ | _____ | 7. absolute | _____ | _____ |
| 8. attain | _____ | _____ | 8. intermittent | _____ | _____ |
| 9. rehearse | _____ | _____ | 9. precipitation | _____ | _____ |
| 10. theoretical | _____ | _____ | 10. residue | _____ | _____ |
| 11. potential | _____ | _____ | 11. asphalt | _____ | _____ |
| 12. cremation | _____ | _____ | 12. dishonorable | _____ | _____ |
| 13. mystic | _____ | _____ | 13. martial | _____ | _____ |
| 14. trudge | _____ | _____ | 14. chronological | _____ | _____ |
| 15. pulp | _____ | _____ | 15. phantom | _____ | _____ |
| 16. fickle | _____ | _____ | 16. ardent | _____ | _____ |
| 17. subside | _____ | _____ | 17. congested | _____ | _____ |
| 18. institution | _____ | _____ | 18. imploringly | _____ | _____ |
| 19. diverge | _____ | _____ | 19. obsolete | _____ | _____ |
| 20. fundamental | _____ | _____ | 20. remote | _____ | _____ |

Number Correct _____ _____        Number Correct _____ _____

Total Score _____        Total Score _____

## Scoring Guide for Graded Word Lists

| Independent | Instructional | Frustration |
|---|---|---|
| 20 19 | 18 17 16 15 14 | 13 or less |

F  1. ___ What were the children's names?
          (Tom and Beth)

F  2. ___ What was the first thing they saw?
          (the band)

E  3. ___ Why did Tom jump up and down?
          (any logical response; he was excited; he
          couldn't see)

I  4. ___ What were the children probably doing?
          (watching a parade)

V  5. ___ What is a "band"?
          (a group of people with instruments)

"Here it comes!" said Tom.

"I can see it," said Beth. "Here comes the band!"

Tom jumped up and down. "Look at the man. He is funny. I can see his red hat."

"Look!" said Beth. "I see a dog. Here comes a car. It is big. This is fun!"

Percent of Comprehension ____

Percent of Word Recognition ____

____ WPM
) 3000

## Scoring Guide: Pre-Primer

Percent of Word Recognition in Context

| 100 99 | 98 97 96 | 95 | 94 93 92 91 | 90 or less |
|---|---|---|---|---|
| Independent Level | Independent or Instructional | Instructional Level | Instructional or Frustration | Frustration Level |
| 100 95 90 | 85 80 | 75 | 70 65 60 55 | 50 or less |

Percent of Comprehension

C

M  1. ___  What is this story about?
           (feeding the hungry birds)

F  2. ___  Who was in this story?
           (Jim and Meg; two children)

F  3. ___  What did the children see in the snow?
           (birds)

F  4. ___  What did the birds want?
           (food)

F  5. ___  Why couldn't the birds find any food?
           (the snow was deep)

F  6. ___  Where did the children get the food for
           the birds?
           (from their mother)

I  7. ___  What season of the year is it?
           (winter)

I  8. ___  What do you think the birds did after
           they finished the bread?
           (any logical response)

E  9. ___  How do you think the children felt
           about the hungry birds? Why?
           (any logical response)

V 10. ___  What does "find" mean?
           (to find something; to see)

Percent of Comprehension _____

"See the small birds," said Jim.

"They are looking in the snow. They want

food."

"The snow is deep," said Meg. "They

cannot find food."

Jim said, "Let's help them."

"Yes," said Meg. "We can get bread

for them."

Jim and Meg ran home. They asked

Mother for bread. Mother gave bread to

them. Then they ran to find the birds.

"There are the birds," said Meg.

"Give them the bread."

Jim put the bread on the snow.

Meg said, "Look at the birds! They

are eating the bread."

"They are happy now," said Jim.

"They are fat and happy."

Percent of Word Recognition _____

_____ WPM
)‾6000

## Scoring Guide: Primer

Percent of Word Recognition in Context

| 100 99 | 98 97 96 | 95 | 94 93 92 91 | 90 or less |
|---|---|---|---|---|
| Independent Level | Independent or Instructional | Instructional Level | Instructional or Frustration | Frustration Level |
| 100 95 90 | 85 80 | 75 | 70 65 60 55 | 50 or less |

Percent of Comprehension

M 1. ___ What is this story about?
(boys raking and playing or jumping in leaves)

F 2. ___ Who was in this story?
(Bill and Pat; two boys)

F 3. ___ What did the boys do with the leaves?
(raked them; jumped or dived in them; threw them about)

F 4. ___ What was Bill's idea?
(to jump in the big pile of leaves)

F 5. ___ What did Pat do?
(he jumped into the pile too)

F 6. ___ What happened to the pile of leaves?
(it was scattered all over the yard; the boys messed it up)

I 7. ___ What season do you think it was? Why?
(any logical response; fall)

I 8. ___ Why did Mother ask if she heard only two boys?
(any logical response; they made a lot of noise)

E 9. ___ How do you think Mother felt about what the boys were doing?
(any logical response)

V 10. ___ What is "diving"?
(jumping or falling in head first)

Percent of Comprehension ___

Bill had many leaves in his yard. Bill raked them into a big pile. Pat helped.

Then Bill got a very good idea.

He ran and jumped in that pile of leaves.

"Wow! What fun!"

"Let me jump," said Pat. So he jumped in too.

Soon both boys were diving in. They threw leaves into the air.

Mother looked out and said, "I see two boys having fun. Do I hear only *two* boys?"

"See our big pile!" said Bill.

"Where?" asked Mother.

The boys looked around. The pile was not big now. The leaves were all over the yard.

Percent of Word Recognition ___

___WPM
$\overline{)6000}$

### Scoring Guide: One

Percent of Word Recognition in Context

| 100 99 | 98 97 96 | 95 | 94 93 92 91 | 90 or less |
|---|---|---|---|---|
| Independent Level | Independent or Instructional | Instructional Level | Instructional or Frustration | Frustration Level |
| 100 95 90 | 85 80 | 75 | 70 65 60 55 | 50 or less |

Percent of Comprehension

M   1. ___   What is this story about?
(Bob and the zoo)

F   2. ___   What does Bob do?
(takes care of all types of animals at the zoo)

F   3. ___   Where do the animals come from?
(all over the world)

F   4. ___   What did Bob feed the seal and lion?
(fish to the seal and meat to the lion)

F   5. ___   Who takes care of sick animals?
(zoo doctor)

F   6. ___   What does Bob do when the people go home?
(locks the gates and goes home)

I   7. ___   How does Bob know what to feed the animals?
(any logical response)

I   8. ___   How do you think Bob became interested in animals?
(any logical response)

E   9. ___   Why do you think Bob works at the zoo?
(any logical response; because he likes animals)

V   10. ___   What is "raw" meat?
(meat that is not cooked)

Percent of Comprehension ____

Bob works at the zoo. He takes care of all kinds of animals. The animals are brought to the zoo from all over the world. Bob gives hay to the elephant. He feeds raw meat to the lion and fresh fish to the seal. He knows just what to give every animal. Each day Bob washes the cages in the zoo. When an animal gets sick, Bob takes it to the zoo doctor. He will make it well. Bob keeps the zoo keys. When the people go home, Bob locks the gates to the zoo. Then he can go home.

Percent of Word Recognition ____

____ WPM
$)6000$

### Scoring Guide: Two

Percent of Word Recognition in Context

| 100 99 | 98 97 96 | 95 | 94 93 92 91 | 90 or less |
|---|---|---|---|---|
| Independent Level | Independent or Instructional | Instructional Level | Instructional or Frustration | Frustration Level |
| 100 95 90 | 85 80 | 75 | 70 65 60 55 | 50 or less |

Percent of Comprehension

M 1. ___ What is this story about?
(Sally and her parents buying a poodle;
a trip to the pet shop)

F 2. ___ Where did Sally and her parents go?
(to the pet shop)

F 3. ___ What did Sally and her parents see?
(fish, turtles, canaries, cats, and dogs
[any two])

F 4. ___ What did the poodle look like?
(small, furry, black [any two])

F 5. ___ What did the poodle do when Sally
petted it?
(it sat up and begged)

F 6. ___ Why did Sally and her parents laugh?
(the poodle looked so cute)

I 7. ___ Why do you think Sally and her
parents chose the poodle?
(any logical response; it was a smart
dog; it was cute)

I 8. ___ Why do you think Sally wanted a dog?
(any logical response; she liked dogs;
she didn't have anyone to play with)

E 9. ___ What will they do with the dog once
they get it home?
(any logical response)

V 10. ___ What does "bouncing" mean?
(to spring back; to go up and down)

Percent of Comprehension ____

Sally really wanted a little dog. One day she went with her parents to the pet shop. They looked at the fish, turtles, canaries, cats, and, of course, dogs. Sally and her parents saw one nice puppy that acted very lively. It looked like a small bouncing black ball of fur. The puppy was a fluffy black poodle. It jumped around in its cage. When Sally petted the puppy, it sat up and begged. Sally and her parents laughed because the poodle looked so cute. They decided to buy the poddle. After all, who could resist such a smart dog?

Percent of Word Recognition ____

$\frac{\qquad \text{WPM}}{)6000}$

## Scoring Guide: Three

Percent of Word Recognition in Context

| 100 99 | 98 97 96 | 95 | 94 93 92 91 | 90 or less |
|---|---|---|---|---|
| Independent Level | Independent or Instructional | Instructional Level | Instructional or Frustration | Frustration Level |
| 100 95 90 | 85 80 | 75 | 70 65 60 55 | 50 or less |

Percent of Comprehension

M   1. ___ What is this story about?
(a forest fire)

F   2. ___ What was unusual about this summer?
(it had been a dry one)

F   3. ___ What did the animals try to do?
(escape; warn each other)

F   4. ___ What was heard and seen in the woods
before the fire began?
(thunder and lightning)

F   5. ___ What colors were the burning trees?
(yellow and red)

F   6. ___ Why was it difficult for the animals to
breathe?
(the smoke filled the air)

I   7. ___ Why had the trees died?
(any logical response; it had been a dry
summer)

I   8. ___ What probably started the fire?
(lightning)

E   9. ___ What problems do you think the
surviving animals might have?
(any logical response)

V   10. ___ What does "wilted" mean?
(withered; limp; dying)

Percent of Comprehension ____

The summer had been a dry one, unusual for this area. Trees and bushes in the forest wilted and died. One afternoon it began to rain. A storm descended upon the forest. Thunder and lightning were heard and seen in the forest. Suddenly a spark touched the dry leaves and a fire began. The animals warned each other as they hurried to escape the flames. As the fire came closer, trees fell to the ground. Their branches were yellow and red. The smoke was so thick the animals could hardly breathe. Many could not escape the danger of the flames.

Percent of Word Recognition ____

____ WPM
$\overline{)6000}$

## Scoring Guide: Four

### Percent of Word Recognition in Context

| 100 99 | 98 97 96 | 95 | 94 93 92 91 | 90 or less |
|---|---|---|---|---|
| Independent Level | Independent or Instructional | Instructional Level | Instructional or Frustration | Frustration Level |
| 100 95 90 | 85 80 | 75 | 70 65 60 55 | 50 or less |

Percent of Comprehension

127

M 1. ____ What does this story describe?
(work the settlers did to build a house)

F 2. ____ Why did the settlers have to build their own houses?
(there were no special people to do it)

F 3. ____ What jobs did the men do?
(cut the trees and built the frame of the house)

F 4. ____ What was the women's work?
(to feed the men)

F 5. ____ Where did the women place the food?
(on tables outside)

F 6. ____ What did the older children do?
(carted bits of wood; helped the women)

I 7. ____ Why did so many people work together?
(any logical response)

I 8. ____ What do you think was the hardest job?
(any logical response)

E 9. ____ Which job would you pick? Why?
(any logical response)

V 10. ____ What does "tedious" mean?
(dull; tiring)

Percent of Comprehension ____

When the first settlers came to America, there were no special men to build houses, so they did the work themselves. All the people in the area would come and help. Some men would cut the trees and others would take this wood and start forming the frame of the house. The work was tedious and long and gave the men enormous appetites. Feeding them was the women's work. They brought large quantities of food and set it outside on long wooden tables. The older children assisted by carting bits of wood or helping the women. The younger children played.

Percent of Word Recognition ____

$$\frac{\text{____WPM}}{6000}$$

**Scoring Guide: Five**
Percent of Word Recognition in Context

| 100 99 | 98 97 96 | 95 | 94 93 92 91 | 90 or less |
|---|---|---|---|---|
| Independent Level | Independent or Instructional | Instructional Level | Instructional or Frustration | Frustration Level |
| 100 95 90 | 85 80 | 75 | 70 65 60 55 | 50 or less |

Percent of Comprehension

C 6687

M   1. ___ What is this paragraph about?
(sunflowers)

F   2. ___ How did the sunflower get its name?
(turning its head to face the sun)

F   3. ___ How tall is the sunflower?
(three to fifteen feet)

F   4. ___ What color are the outer petals?
(yellow)

F   5. ___ What color is the inner circle of the
sunflower?
(brown)

F   6. ___ What is the head of the sunflower
similar to?
(daisy)

I   7. ___ Would some sunflowers be taller than
you are? Why?
(any logical response)

I   8. ___ What do you think happens to the
seeds?
(any logical response)

E   9. ___ Name some qualities you think make
the sunflower a strong plant.
(any logical response)

V  10. ___ What does "unique" patterns mean?
(different arrangements)

Percent of Comprehension ____

Among the most amazing flowers found in the Midwest is the sunflower. Legend states that the flower got its name from its strange habit of turning its head in order to face the sun all day. The sunflower is a very strong plant ranging in height from three to fifteen feet. The head of the sunflower is like that of the daisy. Both have an outer circle of wide yellow petals and an inner circle of small brown flowers. Seeds later form from these small flowers. These seeds produce some of the most unique patterns found in the plant world.

Percent of Word Recognition ____

____ WPM
$\overline{)6000}$

## Scoring Guide: Six

Percent of Word Recognition in Context

| 100 99 | 98 97 96 | 95 | 94 93 92 91 | 90 or less |
|---|---|---|---|---|
| Independent Level | Independent or Instructional | Instructional Level | Instructional or Frustration | Frustration Level |
| 100 95 90 | 85 80 | 75 | 70 65 60 55 | 50 or less |

Percent of Comprehension

M  1. ___  What is the main idea of this paragraph?
(Indians worshipped power in things of nature)

F  2. ___  Why did the Indians hold festivals?
(to honor the Great Spirit)

F  3. ___  How did the Indians decorate themselves for the festivals?
(painted their faces and bodies; wore their best clothes)

F  4. ___  What did the medicine man do?
(led them in the celebration)

F  5. ___  What were the Indians doing at their festivals?
(dancing and feasting)

F  6. ___  What did the braves pray for?
(a sign from the Great Spirit)

I  7. ___  What do you think the Indians wanted from the Great Spirit?
(any logical response)

I  8. ___  Why do you think the medicine man would lead the celebration?
(any logical response)

E  9. ___  Why do you think the Indians worshipped things of nature?
(any logical response)

V  10. ___  What is meant by "visible"?
(can be seen)

Percent of Comprehension ____

Indians worshipped the power in natural things, such as the stars, moon, and the sun. At various times during the year they would hold festivals in honor of this power that they named the Great Spirit. On those occasions they would have ceremonies of dancing and feasting. The braves would decorate their bodies and faces and dress themselves in their best clothes. A medicine man would lead them in the celebration that continued for several days. While gathered about the council fire, the braves prayed that the Great Spirit would reveal his wish for them by sending some sign.

Percent of Word Recognition ____

$6000 \overline{)\phantom{xxx}} $ WPM

### Scoring Guide: Seven

Percent of Word Recognition in Context

| 100 99 | 98 97 96 | 95 | 94 93 92 91 | 90 or less |
|---|---|---|---|---|
| Independent Level | Independent or Instructional | Instructional Level | Instructional or Frustration | Frustration Level |
| 100 95 90 | 85 80 | 75 | 70 65 60 55 | 50 or less |

Percent of Comprehension

**C 1883**

M    1. ___ What is this selection about?
(man's interdependence with his environment)

F    2. ___ What does modern man use to change the environment?
(science and technology)

F    3. ___ Why is man able to investigate the environment?
(he has a brain)

F    4. ___ What are synthetic fibers made from?
(matter found in the environment)

F    5. ___ What are some of the things in the environment which man uses?
(plants, animals, wood, cotton, and wool [any two])

F    6. ___ What does man use to make his shirts?
(fiber from the cotton plant)

I    7. ___ What are some of the ways in which man and the environment are interdependent?
(any logical response)

I    8. ___ How do you think man has been able to make so much progress?
(any logical response)

E    9. ___ Do you think it's a good thing for man to change his environment?
(any logical response)

V   10. ___ What does "synthetic" mean?
(manmade; made from several things put together)

Percent of Comprehension ____

Besides using plants and animals for food, man uses the hides of animals for shoes, the wood from trees to build houses, the fiber from the cotton plant to make his shirts, and the wool from sheep to make his suits and coats. Even the synthetic fibers that man uses are made from matter found in the environment.

Man and his environment are interdependent, but that is not the whole story. Modern man can do much more; he uses science and technology to change his environment. Because of his brain, man can investigate his environment and sometimes change it.

Percent of Word Recognition ____

____ WPM
$\overline{)6000}$

### Scoring Guide: Eight

Percent of Word Recognition in Context

| 100 99 | 98 97 96 | 95 | 94 93 92 91 | 90 or less |
|---|---|---|---|---|
| Independent Level | Independent or Instructional | Instructional Level | Instructional or Frustration | Frustration Level |
| 100 95 90 | 85 80 | 75 | 70 65 60 55 | 50 or less |

Percent of Comprehension

# APPENDICES

# APPENDIX A

## Sources for Further Learning

A search of the literature dealing with informal reading inventories (IRIs) uncovered over one hundred pertinent articles and research studies. The brief annotated bibliography that follows contains a carefully selected portion of those sources. It is believed that these annotations accurately represent a good overview of the development and use of IRIs, current research, and future directions.

### Overview

Beldin, H. O. "Informal Reading Testing: Historical Review and Review of the Research." In William K. Durr (ed.), *Reading Difficulties: Diagnosis, Correction, and Remediation.* Newark, Delaware: International Reading Association, 1970, 67–84.

Presents an historical overview of the literature regarding the analysis of reading performance. The author examines pertinent research from the 1900s to the 1960s for specific contributions to IRIs. Research and conclusions on criteria, sources of test materials, and evaluations of word perception errors are cited. A list of references that have influenced the development of IRIs is included.

Guszak, Frank J. "Dilemmas in Informal Reading Assessments," *Elementary English,* 47 (May, 1970), 666–70.

Includes a brief discussion of general aspects of IRIs and focuses upon some of the difficulties inherent in their use, notably the unresolved concern over word recognition, comprehension, and fluency determinants. Several research questions are posed which the author considers implicit to determining the validity of various factors and concepts involved in the use of IRIs.

Johns, Jerry L.; Sharon Garton; Paula Schoenfelder; and Patricia Skriba (comp.). *Assessing Reading Behavior: Informal Reading Inventories* (An Annotated Bibliography). Newark, Delaware: International Reading Association, 1977.

Presents and categorizes over one hundred annotations relevant to the development, use, and interpretation of IRIs. The compilers have divided the entries into five major categories: (1) basic information on IRIs; (2) dilemmas associated with IRIs; (3) comparisons between IRIs and standardized tests; (4) pyscholinguistic insights into reading errors; and (5) factors related to IRI usage. A brief introduction delineates major trends and offers additional insights. The compilers endeavor to describe the values of IRIs and the difficulties inherent in their use.

Pikulski, John. "A Critical Review: Informal Reading Inventories," *The Reading Teacher,* 28 (November, 1974), 141–51.

Discusses the early history of informal diagnostic procedures, points out the continued existence of several perplexing problems regarding the use of IRIs, and reviews some possible solutions. Specific facets discussed are the establishment of levels, evaluation of validity and reliability, use of quantitative or qualitative criteria, and the type of questions which should be included. The author also describes a study concerning the criteria for selecting the instructional level.

## Utilization

Betts, Emmett Albert. *Foundations of Reading Instruction.* New York: American Book Company, 1954.

Chapter 21 deals with specific reading needs and includes very specific and detailed information on IRIs. Inventories are discussed in terms of uses, basic assumptions, reading levels, construction, general administration procedures, limitations, and advantages. The chapter includes examples of separate checklists that can be used by experienced and inexperienced examiners to record observations made during IRI administrations and also includes a summary form which was used in the author's reading clinic.

Geeslin, Robert H. "The Placement Inventory Alternative," *The Reading Teacher,* 25 (January, 1972), 332–35.

Suggests that the placement inventory is the most practical and efficient technique for determining a student's functional reading level. Eight steps outline the suggested method for administering the placement inventory. The author also discusses the usefulness of observing student anxiety during the reading situation and notes that frustration is manifested by a dramatic rise in miscuing, usually evidenced as the student exceeds a 10 percent error rate.

Goodman, Yetta M. "Using Children's Reading Miscues for New Teaching Srategies," *The Reading Teacher,* 23 (February, 1970), 455–59.

Discusses procedures for making use of children's miscues to aid reading instruction. The view that certain miscues are of a higher order than others is presented. Teachers are encouraged to handle their students' errors instructionally through provisions for teaching-learning strategies.

Hollander, Sheila K. "Why's a Busy Teacher Like You Giving an IRI?" *Elementary English,* 51 (September, 1974), 905–7.

Encourages the busy teacher to consider the benefits that can be derived from the administration of an IRI and, further, to compare these results with those obtained from a standardized test. The author contends that IRIs are more valid than standardized instruments for assessing a child's reading level and suggests practical procedures for using IRIs in the classroom.

Johns, Jerry L. "Matching Students with Books," *Contemporary Education,* 48 (Spring, 1977), 133–38.

Contends that giving students books of appropriate difficulty may improve reading instruction and recommends the use of IRIs, supported by teacher judgment, for matching students with books. The author explains how results from the administration of an IRI can be used to enhance instruction. A chart summarizing nine published reading inventories is included.

Johnson, Marjorie Seddon and Roy A. Kress. *Informal Reading Inventories.* Newark, Delaware: International Reading Association, 1965.

Discusses techniques for developing and using IRIs. The idea that teaching provides many opportunities for informal diagnosis and evaluation is presented, along with notions regarding the implementation of this concept. Detailed procedures for group and individual inventories are delineated.

McCracken, Robert A. "The Informal Reading Inventory as a Means of Improving Instruction." In Thomas C. Barrett (ed.), *Perspectives in Reading: The Evaluation of Children's Reading Achievement.* Newark, Delaware: International Reading Association, 1967, 79–96.

Presentation is organized into two main thrusts. The first emphasis defines an IRI, tells how to administer it, and states objective standards for evaluating its results. The second thrust deals with the use of IRI results in the classroom. The author does not view the IRI as a diagnostic tool, but rather as a placement tool.

McGinnis, Dorothy J. "Making the Most of Informal Inventories." In Dorothy L. DeBoer (ed.), *Reading Diagnosis and Evaluation,* 1968 Proceedings, Volume 13, Part 4. Newark, Delaware: International Reading Association, 1970, 93–99.

Suggests that reading and nonreading areas can be observed and evaluated through the perceptive use of informal inventories. The author defines informal inventories, points out the importance of careful observations, and indicates how observations may lead to "hunches" regarding the causes of a student's reading difficulties. A list of inferences made from observations of a specific student is provided for evaluation.

Valmont, William J. "Creating Questions for Informal Reading Inventories," *The Reading Teacher,* 25 (March, 1972), 509–12.

Proposes that designing and constructing an IRI increases its value to the user. Particularly important in an IRI is the quality of its questions. Based upon his experience, the author offers twenty specific guidelines in the preparation of questions for an IRI. The types of questions described include main idea, detail, inference, drawing conclusions, organization, cause and effect, and vocabulary. Helpful examples are given for each type of question.

## Research on Reading Levels

Ekwall, Eldon E. "Informal Reading Inventories: The Instructional Level," *The Reading Teacher,* 29 (April, 1976), 662–65.

Deals with the confusion and misunderstanding over the instructional level in reading and attempts to clarify what is meant by the instructional level according to authors such as Johnson and Kress. Evidence is presented in support of the original criteria for frustration and independent levels. The author concludes that the original criteria given by Betts and by Johnson and Kress are approximately correct if repetitions are counted as errors.

Hays, Warren S. "Criteria for the Instructional Level of Reading," 1975. Microfiche ED 117 665.

Reports a study designed to answer two general questions concerning the instructional level of reading: (1) What percentage of word recognition must second and fifth graders maintain in order to achieve a certain percentage of comprehension? (2) Are those word recognition percentages the same for both groups? Twenty-five second and twenty-five fifth graders were randomly selected from three middle-class schools. An IRI was developed and administered to each subject. The data were analyzed and median word recognition scores were computed across levels of readability for various bands of comprehension. Subjects were asked to read two comparable passages at each level, one orally at sight and the other silently at sight. The results indicated that most second and fifth graders needed to achieve a word recognition score of at least 98 or 99 percent on the oral passage in order to have an accompanying comprehension score of at least 75 percent on the silent passage. Most second graders who achieved less than 92 percent recognition had accompanying comprehension of less than 50 percent. Most fifth graders who achieved less than 96 percent recognition had accompanying comprehension scores of less than 50 percent. The author questions using the 95 percent word recognition criterion for the instructional level.

Kender, Joseph P. and Herbert Rubenstein. "Recall Versus Reinspection in IRI Comprehension Tests," *The Reading Teacher,* 30 (April, 1977), 776–79.

Maintains that recall-type questions may merely test an individual's ability to remember what has been read rather than to understand it. Describes a study of thirty-two fourth graders, sixteen of high reading ability and sixteen of low reading ability, which attempted to compare an IRI comprehension check by means of recall questions with a check by means of reinspection. The study was designed to determine: (1) the difference, if any, between recall scores and reinspection scores; and (2) whether memory for sentence content is an intrinsic part of reading comprehension. To test the hypotheses, subjects read two IRI passages at each level of difficulty; comprehension was checked by means of recall for one passage and by reinspection for the other. Findings included that: (1) reinspection scores were significantly higher than recall scores for both groups; and (2) the effect of reinspection was substantially the same for both ability groups. Concludes that readers should be allowed to reinspect IRI passages before answering comprehension questions.

Lowell, Robert E. "Problems in Identifying Reading Levels with Informal Reading Inventories." In William K. Durr (ed.), *Reading Difficulties: Diagnosis, Correction, and Remediation.* Newark, Delaware: International Reading Association, 1970, 120–26.

Buffets the concept of the independent, instructional, and frustration levels by presenting various arguments and citing supportive evidence. Weaknesses external to and inherent in the testing procedures may be strong enough to invalidate the concepts upon which IRIs are built. Teachers may have predetermined biases about reading levels and may have a poor concept of the reading process. The author further points out that the distinctions between the three levels may be too fine. In relation to the main testing technique of oral reading, the author states three objections: (1) oral reading at sight is contrary to classroom practice and may not be a valid testing tool; (2) judging word errors, noting phrasing and symptoms of difficulty may present discrepancies; and (3) oral reading improves with rereading or preparation. Which performance should be used as adequacy of performance? Reading performance is also influenced by content and potential interest of a selection and the individual's desire to read. A suggestion is made that more attention be given to reader interest and less to examiner judgment, finely differentiated levels of performance, and oral reading.

Powell, William R. and Colin G. Dunkeld. "Validity of the IRI Reading Levels," *Elementary English,* 48 (October, 1971), 637–42.

Focuses on the discrepancies between various sets of criteria by which different authorities define the instructional level. The authors also seek to offer congruent validity for a set of criteria, at least as far as the dimension of word recognition miscues is concerned. The authors contend that the instructional level as designated by the IRI is an unvalidated construct. Previously, the authors held the position that as long as 70 to 75 percent comprehension was maintained, the word recognition error patterns could be tolerated. Observation, however, gave rise to the thought that word recognition criteria may be a function of the difficulty of materials and the age/grade of the child. An investigation using eight sets of criteria was offered for comparison. Standardized oral tests provided the data for five of these sets of criteria. Conclusions tend to support the disuse of the Betts criteria (word recognition of 95 percent). Criteria which attempted to reflect the progression of the increase of language difficulty and the reader's response to this increase appear to be more suitable. Powell and Dunkeld state that their criteria more nearly resemble children's actual performance, though all criteria need further verification.

## Comparisons with Standardized Tests

Johns, Jerry L. "Can Teachers Use Standardized Reading Tests to Determine Students' Instructional Levels?" *Illinois School Research,* 11 (Spring, 1975), 29–35.

Evaluates a procedure, outlined by Farr and Anastasiow in an IRA Service Bulletin, whereby a teacher may use standardized test scores to determine a student's reading levels, provided some IRIs are administered and a relationship is established between the two test scores. The author describes a study using the Classroom Reading Inventory and Survey D of the Gates-MacGinitie Reading Tests with a fourth grade class to assess the practicality of this approach. The study did not confirm that this procedure can be used to place the students at their instructional levels accurately. The need for further study in this area is stressed.

McCracken, Robert A. "Standardized Reading Tests and Informal Reading Inventories," *Education,* 82 (February, 1962), 366–69.

Reports and discusses a study conducted to compare the grade level ratings of fifty-six sixth grade students on the Iowa Test of Basic Skills and the reading levels attained on an IRI. The study found that the grade levels obtained on the standardized test were approximately two years higher than the IRI instructional ratings. The author concludes that care must be exercised when interpreting the scores of standardized reading tests.

Oliver, Jo Ellen and Richard D. Arnold. "Comparing a Standardized Test, an Informal Inventory and Teacher Judgment on Third Grade Reading," *Reading Improvement,* 15 (Spring, 1978), 56–59.

Compares the results of the Iowa Test of Basic Skills, teacher judgments, and the Goudy Informal Reading Inventory, using thirty third grade students. Without knowledge of the test scores, teachers estimated instructional reading levels. The means of teacher judgment and standardized test scores were not significantly different; however, the mean of IRI placement was significantly different ($p < .01$) from teacher judgment and standardized test score means. The highest correlation (.81) was found between teacher judgment and the IRI results. Scores from the IRI placed students in easier materials than either standardized test scores or teacher judgment. The authors also review previous research comparing IRIs and standardized tests.

Sipay, Edward R. "A Comparison of Standardized Reading Scores and Functional Reading Levels," *The Reading Teacher,* 17 (January, 1964), 265–68.

Describes a study that attempted to compare objectively the extent to which reading achievement, as measured by three different standardized reading achievement tests, differed from the reading level as estimated by two forms of an IRI. Even though standardized reading achievement tests and IRIs are frequently employed to estimate a child's level of reading achievement, a review of the literature reveals differing opinions among reading authorities regarding the relationship of standardized test scores and functional reading levels. The author concludes that it is impossible to generalize whether standardized reading test scores tend to indicate instructional or frustration level since one must consider the test used and the criteria employed to estimate functional reading levels.

## Future Directions

Smith, Laura and Constance Weaver. "A Psycholinguistic Look at the Informal Reading Inventory Part I: Looking at the Quality of Readers' Miscues: A Rationale and an Easy Method," *Reading Horizons,* 19 (Fall, 1978), 12–22.

Encourages IRI users to conduct a qualitative rather than a quantitative analysis of readers' miscues. Reading for meaning is emphasized, as is the effectiveness of teaching word analysis skills through the use of context. The article includes a simplified version of Goodman and Burke's Reading Miscue Inventory procedure for analyzing a reader's miscues. Guidelines for obtaining and analyzing a reading sample are offered.

Weaver, Constance and Laura Smith. "A Psycholinguistic Look at the Informal Reading Inventory Part II: Inappropriate Inferences from an Informal Reading Inventory," *Reading Horizons,* 19 (Winter, 1979), 103–11.

Advises teachers to regard tests that measure a reader's recognition of words in isolation with caution because such tests commonly underestimate the reader's ability to process contextual material. The authors suggest that the use of a simplified version of Goodman and Burke's miscue analysis may be preferable to the use of most available IRIs. An advantage of the miscue analysis procedure lies in its applicability to instructional planning. The importance of evaluating the reader's strengths as well as weaknesses is emphasized.

Williamson, Leon E. and Freda Young. "The IRI and RMI Diagnostic Concepts Should be Synthesized," *Journal of Reading Behavior,* 5 (July, 1974), 183–94.

Summarizes ten advantages of the IRI and nine questions used to evaluate a reader's errors (miscues) in the Reading Miscue Inventory (RMI). The authors hypothesize that in synthesizing the RMI concepts with those of IRIs, the advantages of each are enhanced because the RMI questions focus on quality rather than quantity. "To understand quantity, quality must be examined in quantitative units." The authors support the thought that reading errors are powerful cues to use in diagnosing reading performance. Thirty intermediate-grade students were tested; their miscues, analyzed according to the RMI, exhibited reading behaviors different at instructional and frustration levels. Specific behaviors typical of each level are presented in charts and discussions. The conclusions support a synthesis of the concepts underlying IRIs and the RMI.

# APPENDIX B

# Sample Reading Strategy Lessons*

---

**SITUATION 1**

The student repeats words, phrases, or sentences.

---

## Comment and Strategies

Such repetitions may help the student to get meaning. The teacher must decide whether the student is anticipating a "hard" word, making a legitimate effort to have the reading make sense, or merely repeating from habit. Consider the following:

1. If the student's repetitions are frequent, it is possible that the reading materials are too difficult. If this is the case, provide the student with reading materials at his instructional level.
2. Repetitions that are "stalls" may provide additional time to unlock an unknown word. This may be a normal part of the reading process. Excessive use of the "stall" technique, however, may indicate that the reading material is too difficult and/or effective reading strategies are needed. It may also indicate a need to teach how the flow of language can be used to anticipate words.
3. Praise the student when he repeats a word, phrase, or sentence to preserve ongoing meaning. Tell the student that such behavior is fully acceptable when the reading doesn't make sense. Provide examples similar to the following that a student and/or class can discuss and evaluate.

    ©*They) grew*
    He knew he must try to save the woods he loved so much.

    © *in)*
    He jumped on the high wall perfectly.

4. If repetitions are merely a habit, it may be helpful to have the student record his reading on a tape recorder and then discuss it with the teacher. The student should note that the majority of the repetitions are a habit which do not generally result in an effective reading strategy.

---

**SITUATION 2**

The student waits to be told unknown words; he does not attempt them on his own.

---

## Comment and Strategies

Wait *ten* or *fifteen seconds* and see if this will suggest to the student that you expect him to attempt the word. If a favorable response is not obtained, try these strategies.

1. Have him continue reading to see if subsequent textual information will help him with the unknown word.

---

*Adapted from: Jerry L. Johns, "Strategies for Oral Reading Behavior," *Language Arts,* 52 (November/December, 1975), 1104–07. Copyright © 1975 by the National Council of Teachers of English. Reprinted by permission.

2. Ask the student to go back a line and see if the preceding sentence and the words around the "unknown" word suggest the word. If the student does not suggest a word, ask him to reread the sentence until he makes a good guess.

3. Ask the student to reread the sentence and try to guess a word that begins with the initial sound of the "unknown" word and makes sense.

4. Provide oral examples where the student uses the information provided to anticipate the missing word.

I would like to play _____ .

It's time to go _____ .

I found a _____ in the lawn.

5. Use easy cloze exercises where the student is asked to write in a word that makes sense. Discuss various choices offered by the students. Gradually include some graphic information about the exact word the author used.

---

**SITUATION 3**

The student produces a nonword instead of a real word or omits unknown words.

---

## Comment and Strategies

The student must be helped to realize that reading is a meaningful process and words he says should makes sense. In short, his reading should sound like oral language.

1. Ask the student what his nonword means. It is possible that he has the meaning but has mispronounced the word.

2. Provide oral and written examples where the student attempts to predict the appropriate word that has been omitted.

I will mail the _____ .

The horse _____ over the fence.

3. Provide examples that contain a nonword and ask the student to tell what the nonword could mean.

He drank a glass of *fax*.
The *zop* bought some candy.

4. If the student omits an unknown word, ask him questions like:

Does that sound like language to you?
What word do you think could go in this spot?
Why do you think so?
What word do you know that begins like _____ that would make sense?

If the student is unable to produce a word with the same beginning sound, ask him to try a word that he thinks would make sense.

The goal should be to have the reader aim at producing a word or nonword rather than omitting the word. Remember that there are times when a word can be omitted without a loss in meaning.

---

**SITUATION 4**

The student substitutes words that make sense.

---

## Comment and Strategies

The most important strategy must be enacted by the teacher: remain silent. Try to keep other students from breaking the thought line. You might tell students that readers will sometimes substitute words that make sense. Only those substitutions which do not make sense or alter the meaning should be corrected. To help students decide on substitutions which do or do not make sense, try the following strategies.

1. Provide sentences that contain a substituted word written above the text. Have students discuss whether or not the substituted word makes sense.

   *they*
   They went to the zoo because there were many things to see.

2. Provide exercises that contain substitutions two different readers made in the same sentence. Discuss which substitution appears to be closer to the author's intended meaning.

   *the*
   Billy decided to ride along a little road.

   *walk*
   Billy decided to ride along a little road.

   **NOTE:** Similar strategies may also be used with omissions. For example:

   He knew that there were (so) many things to see. He remembered how bare and black it (had) looked.

   He gave the boy twenty (five) cents.

---

**SITUATION 5**

The student substitutes words which do not make sense and/or distort the meaning.

---

## Comment and Strategies

Remind the student that reading is a meaning-getting process. (Did that sound right to you?) The student must be taught to use semantic (contextual) cues. Try the following strategies:

1. Remind the student to think while he reads so that he will stop and reread the material if it is not making sense. This student may be viewing reading as a "word calling" process. You may need to develop a concept of reading which involves meaning as the crucial element.

2. Give the student oral exercises in which he identifies words that do not make sense in the context of the sentences or the story. Do similar written exercises. For example:

   The postman delivered the groceries.
   He set his calendar so he would wake up at seven o'clock.
   Bill went to the store to buy some candy for her sister.

3. Give the student oral and written exercises containing closure tasks in which the student anticipates omitted words that make sense. Use the cloze procedure as a teaching technique. Develop the notion that language dictates that only certain types of words can be placed after certain language structures.

   After playing, the children _____ .

   I will see you after _____ .

   He was reading a _____ .

   "I lost my money," _____ Bill.

   The _____ climbed the tree.

4. Use small group activities where certain key words in a story are covered. Elicit responses from the group and have students evaluate the responses. The ultimate criterion is: "Does the word you suggest make sense in the phrase (sentence, paragraph)?" Demonstrate how the flow of the story helps the reader to predict certain words.

5. Keep track of substitutions to see if certain words are habitually associated with other words. Write selections where the grammatical structures make it highly unlikely for the habitual associations to occur. For example:

   <u>was</u> and <u>saw</u>

   Once upon a time there <u>was</u> a girl named Jane. Her hair <u>was</u> long and brown. Jane liked to wear ribbons in her hair. One day, while she <u>was</u> walking downtown, she <u>saw</u> some ribbons in a store window. She <u>saw</u> blue, yellow, and pink ribbons. The blue ribbon <u>was</u> the prettiest, so she bought it.

   <u>in</u> and <u>on</u>

   Jim liked to collect insects. He kept the spiders <u>in</u> a jar <u>on</u> top of his dresser. One Friday, his mother invited some friends to come over for coffee. They were talking <u>in</u> the kitchen. Jim took his jar of spiders <u>into</u> the kitchen and set it <u>on</u> the table. When one lady reached for a cup <u>on</u> the table, she bumped the jar. It landed <u>on</u> the floor. What do you think happened next?

<u>when</u> and <u>then</u>

Jim and his mother had some errands to do. His mother said, "I will get my coat; <u>then</u> I will be ready to go. <u>When</u> you find your jacket, come out to the car. First, we will go to the supermarket; <u>then</u> we can go to the pet shop to find out <u>when</u> the puppy will be ready to come home. <u>When</u> we bring the puppy home you will get the basket out of the closet. <u>Then</u> the puppy will have a nice place to sleep."

**NOTE:** Similar strategies may also be used with omissions that distort the meaning.

---

**SITUATION 6**

The student **habitually** tries to sound out words when confronted with an "unknown" word in a natural reading situation.

---

## Comment and Strategies

Some students may have been taught that the appropriate strategy is to sound out words when they are unknown. Other students may not have been taught any other strategies that can be applied in such a situation. In either case, teachers must help the student to use his knowledge of language (syntax) and teach the value of context (semantic) cues. The following strategies represent a meager but appropriate beginning:

1. Show the student that he can often correctly predict a word in oral language before he hears it. Help him use this same knowledge in his reading. For example:

   He gave the kitten some _____ .

   Put a stamp on the _____ .

   Five pennies make a _____ .

2. Provide examples where two readers have come across the same unknown word. Discuss the responses of the two readers in an attempt to decide which reader has been most effective and the reasons for his effectiveness.

   | | |
   |---|---|
   | Text: | The car went down the old *street*. |
   | Reader 1: | The car went down the old *road*. |
   | Reader 2: | The car went down the old *stream*. |

3. Provide words that the student is probably able to pronounce but that are not familiar in meaning. Then provide a sentence that builds meaning for the word. For example:

   | | |
   |---|---|
   | kingcups | He picked some kingcups for his mother because she likes flowers. |
   | kipper | The kipper is not usually caught by fishermen. |

The teacher might then provide words in the student's meaning vocabulary that he is unable to pronounce. Such words can then be placed in a context that builds meaning for the words. Through such exercises the student should realize that he can get meaning without always sounding out words.

---

**SITUATION 7**

The student ignores punctuation, adds punctuation, or uses inappropriate intonation.

---

## Comment and Strategies

1. The student should be shown examples where punctuation is ignored or substituted. In some cases meaning may not be disturbed; in other cases a change in meaning may be involved. Discuss whether or not the reader should have paid attention to the punctuation. The following examples may be useful:

   He woke up and got ready for school.

   Billy looked ahead and saw smoke coming out of a pile of dry brush.

   Even as Billy looked, the flames burst out.

   But Blaze scrambled up the bank, and Billy held on somehow, his arms around the pony's neck.

   Down Blaze went to his knees, and Billy slipped out of the saddle.

2. Read plays and write experience stories. Help the student see the role of punctuation.
3. Teach the basic marks of punctuation.
4. Discuss reading that has been tape recorded.

# APPENDIX C

## Aids for Analyzing and Summarizing Test Results

**Summary of Criteria for a Student's Reading Levels**

**INDEPENDENT LEVEL:** The student can read the book without difficulty. At this level the student can read books without teacher assistance.

_____ 90% comprehension

_____ 99% pronunciation of words in context

_____ No head movement, vocalizing, finger pointing

_____ Good phrasing, rhythmical oral reading without teacher assistance

**INSTRUCTIONAL LEVEL:** The student can read the book with instruction. At this level the student is challenged by books, but they are not too difficult.

_____ 75% comprehension

_____ 95% pronunciation of words in context

_____ No head movement, vocalizing, finger pointing

_____ Good phrasing

**FRUSTRATION LEVEL:** The student "bogs down" in this book. At this level the student finds books too difficult.

_____ 50% (or less) comprehension

_____ 90% (or less) pronunciation of words in context

_____ Head movement, vocalizing, finger pointing, flushed face—TENSION

_____ Lack of interest, poor attention—FUTILITY

It is important that students be placed in books that will assure them of a successful learning experience as a reward for their efforts!

# QUALITATIVE SUMMARY OF MISCUES ON THE BASIC READING INVENTORY

Jerry L. Johns
Northern Illinois University

| MISCUE | TEXT | GRAPHIC SIMILARITY | | | CONTEXT | | |
| | | Beginning | Middle | End | Acceptable | Unacceptable | Self-Correction |
| --- | --- | --- | --- | --- | --- | --- | --- |
| | | | | | | | |
| | | | | | | | |
| | | | | | | | |
| | | | | | | | |
| | | | | | | | |
| | | | | | | | |
| | | | | | | | |
| | | | | | | | |
| | | | | | | | |
| | | | | | | | |
| | | | | | | | |
| | | | | | | | |
| | | | | | | | |
| | | | | | | | |
| | | | | | | | |
| | | | | | | | |
| | | | | | | | |
| | | | | | | | |
| | | | | | | | |
| | | | | | | | |
| Column Total | | | | | | | |
| Number of Miscues Analyzed | | | | | | | |
| Percentage | | | | | | | |

## PREDICTION STRATEGY

Graphic Similarity

B  M  E

| 100% | | | |
| 90 | | | |
| 80 | | | |
| 70 | | | |
| 60 | | | |
| 50 | | | |
| 40 | | | |
| 30 | | | |
| 20 | | | |
| 10 | | | |

__%  __%  __%

Miscues Acceptable in Context

| 100% | |
| 90 | |
| 80 | |
| 70 | |
| 60 | |
| 50 | |
| 40 | |
| 30 | |
| 20 | |
| 10 | |

__%

## CORRECTION STRATEGY

Unacceptable Miscues Self-Corrected

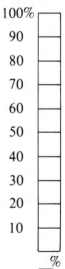

__%

K|H
KENDALL/HUNT PUBLISHING COMPANY
Dubuque, Iowa

# SUMMARY OF STUDENT'S ORAL READING PERFORMANCE
## ON THE BASIC READING INVENTORY

*Jerry L. Johns*
*Northern Illinois University*

| SUMMARY OF STUDENT'S MISCUES IN ORAL READING | | | |
|---|---|---|---|
| Substitutions | | | |
| Different Beginnings | Different Middles | Different Endings | Different in Several Parts |
| | | | |

| Insertions | Omissions | Repetitions | Miscellaneous |
|---|---|---|---|
| | | | |

**KENDALL/HUNT PUBLISHING COMPANY**
Dubuque, Iowa

# SUMMARY OF STUDENT'S COMPREHENSION PERFORMANCE
## ON THE BASIC READING INVENTORY

Jerry L. Johns
Northern Illinois University

| ANALYSIS BY TYPE OF QUESTION | | | | | | | | | | |
|---|---|---|---|---|---|---|---|---|---|---|
| **Grade** | **Fact** | | **Main Idea** | | **Evaluation** | | **Inference** | | **Vocabulary** | |
| | Oral | Silent | Oral | Silent | Oral | Silent | Oral | Silent | Oral | Silent |
| P | ___/5 | ___/5 | ___/1 | ___/1 | ___/1 | ___/1 | ___/2 | ___/2 | ___/1 | ___/1 |
| 1 | ___/5 | ___/5 | ___/1 | ___/1 | ___/1 | ___/1 | ___/2 | ___/2 | ___/1 | ___/1 |
| 2 | ___/5 | ___/5 | ___/1 | ___/1 | ___/1 | ___/1 | ___/2 | ___/2 | ___/1 | ___/1 |
| 3 | ___/5 | ___/5 | ___/1 | ___/1 | ___/1 | ___/1 | ___/2 | ___/2 | ___/1 | ___/1 |
| 4 | ___/5 | ___/5 | ___/1 | ___/1 | ___/1 | ___/1 | ___/2 | ___/2 | ___/1 | ___/1 |
| 5 | ___/5 | ___/5 | ___/1 | ___/1 | ___/1 | ___/1 | ___/2 | ___/2 | ___/1 | ___/1 |
| 6 | ___/5 | ___/5 | ___/1 | ___/1 | ___/1 | ___/1 | ___/2 | ___/2 | ___/1 | ___/1 |
| 7 | ___/5 | ___/5 | ___/1 | ___/1 | ___/1 | ___/1 | ___/2 | ___/2 | ___/1 | ___/1 |
| 8 | ___/5 | ___/5 | ___/1 | ___/1 | ___/1 | ___/1 | ___/2 | ___/2 | ___/1 | ___/1 |
| Ratio Incorrect | ___/___ | ___/___ | ___/___ | ___/___ | ___/___ | ___/___ | ___/___ | ___/___ | ___/___ | ___/___ |
| Percent Incorrect | ___% | ___% | ___% | ___% | ___% | ___% | ___% | ___% | ___% | ___% |
| Average Percent Incorrect | ___% | | ___% | | ___% | | ___% | | ___% | |

| ANALYSIS BY LEVEL OF COMPREHENSION | | | |
|---|---|---|---|
| **Lower-Level Comprehension (Fact Questions Only)** | | **Higher-Level Comprehension (All Other Questions)** | |
| Oral | Silent | Oral | Silent |
| **Ratio Incorrect** ___/___ | ___/___ | ___/___ | ___/___ |
| **Total Ratio Incorrect** ___/___ | | ___/___ | |
| **Total Percent Incorrect** _____% | | _____% | |

**KENDALL/HUNT PUBLISHING COMPANY**
Dubuque, Iowa

# BASIC READING INVENTORY CLASS SUMMARY SHEET

Jerry L. Johns
Northern Illinois University

| Student | Levels | | | | Consistent Strengths (+) and/or Weaknesses (−) | | | | | | | | | | | |
| --- | --- | --- | --- | --- | --- | --- | --- | --- | --- | --- | --- | --- | --- | --- | --- | --- |
| | | | | | Comprehension | | | | | Word Recognition | | | | | | |
| | Ind. | Inst. | Frust. | Lis. | Fact | Main Idea | Inference | Evaluation | Vocabulary | Substitutions | Corrections | Repetitions | Omissions | Punctuation | Phonics | Context |
| | | | | | | | | | | | | | | | | |
| | | | | | | | | | | | | | | | | |
| | | | | | | | | | | | | | | | | |
| | | | | | | | | | | | | | | | | |
| | | | | | | | | | | | | | | | | |
| | | | | | | | | | | | | | | | | |
| | | | | | | | | | | | | | | | | |
| | | | | | | | | | | | | | | | | |
| | | | | | | | | | | | | | | | | |
| | | | | | | | | | | | | | | | | |
| | | | | | | | | | | | | | | | | |
| | | | | | | | | | | | | | | | | |
| | | | | | | | | | | | | | | | | |
| | | | | | | | | | | | | | | | | |
| | | | | | | | | | | | | | | | | |
| | | | | | | | | | | | | | | | | |
| | | | | | | | | | | | | | | | | |
| | | | | | | | | | | | | | | | | |
| | | | | | | | | | | | | | | | | |
| | | | | | | | | | | | | | | | | |
| | | | | | | | | | | | | | | | | |
| | | | | | | | | | | | | | | | | |
| | | | | | | | | | | | | | | | | |
| | | | | | | | | | | | | | | | | |
| | | | | | | | | | | | | | | | | |
| | | | | | | | | | | | | | | | | |
| | | | | | | | | | | | | | | | | |
| | | | | | | | | | | | | | | | | |
| | | | | | | | | | | | | | | | | |
| | | | | | | | | | | | | | | | | |

KH

KENDALL/HUNT PUBLISHING COMPANY
Dubuque, Iowa